The Complete Guide to

SUCCESSFUL
EVENT
PLANNING

with Companion CD-ROM

REVISED 3rd Edition

Shannon C. Kilkenny

The Complete Guide to Successful Event Planning with Companion CD-ROM REVISED 3rd Edition

BUS081000 BUSINESS & ECONOMICS / Industries / Hospitality, Travel & Tourism
BUS007010 BUSINESS & ECONOMICS / Business Communication/ Meetings & Presentations
BUS060000 BUSINESS & ECONOMICS / Small Business

Printed in the United States
BOOK PRODUCTION DESIGN: T.L. Price • design@tlpricefreelance.com

Over the years, we have adopted a number of dogs from rescues and shelters. First there was Bear and after he passed, Ginger and Scout. Now, we have Kira, another rescue. They have brought immense joy and love not just into our lives, but into the lives of all who met them.

We want you to know a portion of the profits of this book will be donated in Bear, Ginger and Scout's memory to local animal shelters, parks, conservation organizations, and other individuals and nonprofit organizations in need of assistance.

– Douglas & Sherri Brown,
President & Vice-President of Atlantic Publishing

Reviews:

"A successful event or seminar takes a clear vision and an enormous amount of planning, details and follow up. Successful Event Planning *is a valuable resource and a "must-have" for any department or organization that puts on events or seminars — regardless of size."*

KAREN R. MCLAUGHLIN, APR, CEO QB COMM, INC., ROCHESTER, NY

"The organization and systems outlined and recommended in this Guide have enabled us to produce greater and more successful events, enhanced the experience for our clients and increased profitability for our business. Kudos to Shannon!"

KATRINKA MCKAY, INNKEEPER AND GENERAL MANAGER, SEBASTOPOL, CA

"Wow! This is what I do for a living!!! It's really gratifying to see things I do daily put into words and even better to know there's a great resource to use when I get stuck."

SIOBHAN COEN, CMP AUTODESK, SAN RAFAEL, CA

"As an event producer for dozens of years, I've found Shannon's complete guide most informative and compelling.... And I thought I knew it all!!!"

META MEHLING META MEHLING & ASSOCIATES, CUPERTINO, CA

"This book explains all of the things that you tend to forget when you plan a large event. It teaches you everything you need to know to put together an unforgettable event, from where to host it, to how to protect your guests, to how to market it. Kilkenny's book also explains how you can save money without compromising the quality of your event, what to do in case of an unforeseen problem, and what to do when the event is over. Simply put, this book really is a complete guide that will teach you everything you need to know about event planning."

TRICIA PSARREAS "TRISH"

"If you know me at all, you may be aware of these two things about me:

1. I like to organize, especially other people.

2. I like to plan and organize events.

Okay, so maybe you've known me for years and never knew that, but now you do. Anyway, I am in the process of planning my boss's inauguration and decided I needed some more event planning resources in my library of books. So I picked up The Complete Guide to Successful Event Planning by Shannon Kilkenny with companion CD-ROM. This morning I popped in the CD-ROM.

Oh.

My.

WORD.

This is an amazing resource...the organizer in me is giddy with excitement! Checklists, Budgets, Event Task Status Reports, Room Set Ups, Speaker Arrangements...it's a plethora of reusable resources right at my fingertips!! Granted, many of these things I have used in the past with events, but oh...to have them easily accessible again...in PDF OR Word format so I can tweak them to my liking...this is almost more exciting than reading the book itself! Timelines. Room Designs. Food and Beverage Servings.

I feel like I've just overdosed on sugar at Willy Wonka's Chocolate Factory or something... bliss..."

SARAH

"Having to plan an event? First-timers or old pros needing a refresher? Go no further than this book. Shannon Kilkenny has outdone herself here with step-by-step instructions and tips to walk you through the whole process of planning and executing even the most difficult event you've ever faced. I found the charts, lists and forms both in the text and the copies on the CD-ROM for easy print out to be the most beneficial.

I think the best thing about this book is that you can take away something from reading the whole book cover to cover. But you can also take away information from individual chapters if the whole book doesn't apply to you."

REBEKAH A. CRAFT

"Whether you are on your first or 500th event, Successful Event Planning is a book that I suggest you have. The plan for success is in your hand. All you have to do is follow it. I have incorporated this information into my project planning for every event. Obviously a true professional wrote this because it's so complete."

KATHERINE LUCAS, REAL ESTATE ENTREPRENEUR NAPLES, FL

"Let's face it. When you're in charge of planning an event — any event — you're the one with the reputation on the line. If the event succeeds or flops, people who were there will remember you. So you can't afford to overlook even the smallest planning detail. You need insurance against failure —and that's where this book comes in!"

"Anyone who's on the hot seat for planning an event can't afford to be more than an arm's length away from Shannon Kilkenny's unmatched expertise".

ROBERT GARDNER

"This book will make your next event planning fantastically easy. I have never seen a better book on how to create the event. It is concise, but no detail or list that you will need is omitted. Its CD-ROM will let you access all the working materials on your computer. It facilitates your creating the ambiance and context you wish to realize through your event. It even helps you "green" your event.

We could say much more but think you will know how great this book is the moment you have your hands on it or view it on this site. The common sense, dedication, and competence of this quite amazing book will grab you right away.

At The Family Institute of Berkeley, we have had to plan many events ranging from small groups to audiences of hundreds including workshop settings, meals, and lodging for people who have come from all over the world over a period of some thirty years. This book would have spared us a lot of inventing and pouring over lists and reminders. You may be able to do all this work yourself but why not have it done for you?

We have worked with Shannon Kilkenny, participated in events and have come to respect and admire her integrity, determination, kindness, and incredible competence. It is that which makes this book uniquely helpful."

ROBERT SHAW, M.D. DIRECTOR, THE FAMILY INSTITUTE OF BERKELEY
JUDITH SHAW, M.A. EDUCATION DIRECTOR AND EVENT COORDINATOR,
THE FAMILY INSTITUTE OF BERKELEY

Author Dedication

To the spirit of my mother, Della, and grandmother, Danny — the ultimate event planners! And my angels extraordinaire!

This one is for you two! And thanks for the happy gene. This nut didn't fall far from your tree.

ndle width (2) 1-tall 5 small
dle Shields   5

ter Lk Stevens Jamie Clark

squet Arlington Nicole Jensen
ande.
ess set Alex Lake Stevens

Princess Wedding -

Fulfillment Center
1388 Bridgewater Rd
Bensalem PA   19020

Ordered By: Fulfillment Center
1388 Bridgewater Rd
BENSALEM, PA
19020

Received By: Robin Thomas
9906 79TH DR NE
MARYSVILLE, WA
98270-7943

Shipping Date	Shipped Via		P.O. #	Order #	
04/11/19	ECONOMY / UM			INGD-FB04595-1	
Product ID	Description		Shipped Qty	Unit Price	Extended Price
9781620231562	90772517 The Complete Guide to		1		

Telephone: Email:

If you have received damaged, defective, or incorrectly shipped merchandise

3"c
cau

$15 Pla
$50 Cr
5
$75 ch

Acknowledgements

This book, many years in the making, is the culmination of my crazy life in the land of hospitality. And what a wild and adventurous event it has been! To those who weaved into and out of my story — I acknowledge each of you, and I honor and appreciate you for enlightening my world. Extraordinary thanks to those who settled in and participated in influencing the person I am today. I am grateful for every encouraging and inspiring word and even the not so positive but truthful and honest evaluations — all were valuable.

A deeply felt thank you to all the readers, past and future, who have interest in pursuing careers in the domain of events. And especially to the professors and teachers who use this book to spread information and education to the young people on the wonderful world of hospitality.

Many thanks to my adventurous partner in life Sande, who has given me the space I need to be me. Thank you for always having my back. And to my lifelong friend Linda Maria (Lord), I so appreciate your time and effort in assisting me in the last gasps of rewriting this book. You are my researcher extraordinaire.

To my esteemed peers and colleagues, thank you. You keep me motivated and challenged to continue rising to any occasion and remind me of what excellence looks like.

And to the storytellers in this book, I honor your time and value your contribution.

We all have choices, so make good ones! Make every day a joyful event!

Table of Contents

SECTION TWO

The Big Picture 47

Chapter 8: Planning for the Environment 89

Chapter 9: Social Responsibility 111

Chapter 10: Culture, Diversity and Ethics 119

SECTION FOUR
High Level Logistics 125

Chapter 11: Get Down to Business 127

Chapter 12: Creating Atmosphere 159

Chapter 13: Food and Beverage Choices 173

SECTION FIVE

Marketing, Networking and Technology 191

Chapter 14: Marketing and Networking....... 193

SECTION SIX
Technology Speaking 213

Chapter 15: The World of Technology 215

Chapter 16: Staying on Top of Technology 217

SECTION SEVEN
Social Media and Social Networking 233

Chapter 17: Using Social Media and Social Networking 235

SECTION EIGHT

Cover Your Assets - Contracts, Insurance and Security 255

Chapter 18: Contracts 257

Chapter 19: Insurance 265

Chapter 20: Security Issues 271

SECTION NINE

On-Site Logistics 279

Chapter 21: Logistically Speaking 281

Chapter 22: The Day Has Arrived! 301

Chapter 23: Wrap It Up!...................313

Chapter 24: Resources...........................319

SECTION TEN

Appendices 325

Appendix A: Tips to Becoming a Great Planner... 327

About This Book

Introduction

Whenever two or more people are gathered, it is an event. Events and event planning have been in existence since the beginning of civilization. One could say that event planning, bringing people together for a specific reason, is the oldest profession in the world. Okay, maybe the second oldest!

In every organization, association, institution, or production company, events are in the process of being planned and executed each and every day. It is a never-ending cycle. The number and variety of events happening daily around the world is staggering. Millions of people are participating in organized events as you read this. Some of these events will be wildly successful and meet their goals and objectives, while others will fall short.

Who is in charge of these thousands of daily events? We are — you and me, the planners, the organizers, the production team and the directors. Whether you are a novice or a well-seasoned event planner, this book is designed to help you become a better organizer and save you time, money and hours of frustration. By using this book to gain new knowledge and learn from others' experiences, you can enjoy your next event just a little more. Event planning is a fun and exciting endeavor. This book is intended to make your life easier by giving you step-by-step guidance.

Maybe you have worked on an event in one capacity or another, either as a volunteer or as a paid employee. Perhaps you participated in planning your high school reunion or a fundraiser for your children's art department. Maybe you did some campaigning for a local politician or planned a seminar to promote your own business. When it was over, did you think of parts of the process that could have gone more smoothly? It's only natural that, in hindsight, we think we could have done this or that to make our life a little easier and our event more successful. This guide is intended to help you with that.

There is no such thing as a perfect or flawless event. Every event will have something go wrong — big or small. Murphy's Law says, "If something can go wrong, it will." Something will be missing, things will change at the last minute, or something unexpected will happen, but a good planner will find the solution and create an illusion so that the people attending the event will never know there was a problem at all. This guide will prepare you for some of those possibilities. They can be as small as forgetting birthday candles for the cake or as big as a hurricane hitting your meeting site for 30,000 participants.

What's New in This Edition?

A lot has happened in the world of events and hospitality since the publishing of my first edition in 2007. The basic guidelines and principals of "how" to plan an event have not really changed. However, changes and improvements in technology, social media and networking, environmental practices, and the importance of cultural sensitivity, diversity and ethics have. Plus, new, healthier ideas for the food and beverage arena have changed enough that a new edition was warranted.

You will find changes in almost every section. Some new stories and mentor moments have been added along with improved ways to make your life as a planner a little bit easier. The biggest changes are in the Technology chapter and the Social Media and Networking section. Technological advances and the Internet world are changing and improving so quickly that by the time you read this, something else will have developed or changed all together. One of our jobs as a planner is to stay on top of these transformations.

In particular, the social media, marketing and networking world has exploded. If you are not part of this phenomenon, it is time to get on board. This new form of business is changing the way we market, connect, plan and meet up with each other. There is so much going on right now that we will only highlight the major social technology. Continue your research and education on your own so that you do not get left behind.

A new chapter has also been added to address cultural sensitivity, diversity and ethics. People around the world continue to migrate, and we are now experiencing a wonderful mix of people and their cultures. This is becoming more common in our everyday lives and certainly in the hospitality world. This isn't new by any means, only more important as we transform what our events are like today — a magnificent assortment of the people of the world.

My Story

When I started in the event planning business many years ago, there were no books or classes on the subject and very few mentors to call upon for advice. There were no professional organizations with tests and certifications or magazines dedicated to the trade. Most events were just assigned to the most reliable person who may or may not have had the time or experience. Fortunately, I loved to gather people. I was a natural, but I had to make my own mistakes and learn hands on, in the moment and standing or running on my own two feet. It was exciting, and I loved it. You have to love it, or do not do it!

I have more than 35 years of experience coordinating events, and I still enjoy it. I have directed, produced and coordinated events in every category of the event industry. There were numerous events in the corporate market, industry shows, spectacular special events and hundreds of social events. Each event was entirely different and prepared me for the next. I learned along the way, mostly through trial and error. Through each job, I learned something new about a different aspect of the trade. It was my path of development that got me here today as an author and speaker.

After this book was published, my career shifted from doing events to speaking to and teaching event planners about events. My speaking path took me all over the United States to speak at Meeting Professionals International (MPI); Meetings, Incentives, Conferences, and Exhibitions (MICE); Hospitality Sales and Marketing Association International (HSMAI); International Special Events Society (ISES); Society of Government Meeting Professionals (SGMP); conferences and conventions; and for private corporations and industries. I have also had the privilege to travel to Kuala Lumpur, Hong Kong, Thailand, and Singapore to share the green message. Visit my website at **www.successfuleventplanning.com**.

This Guide Is For You

Welcome to the fabulous world of event planning! If you have a special event, meeting, concert, conference, festival, seminar, or party to produce, plan, or coordinate, you have come to the right place. Events do not just happen; they are planned, specifically orchestrated, and carefully coordinated. **Preparation is the key to any successful event. Remember, as planners we are responsible for the education, entertainment, feeding, housing, safety and care of all attending or participating in our events.** It is a huge responsibility and not to be taken lightly. This is what you will learn from this guide.

This practical guide is dedicated to saving you time, money, and frustration, without omitting any of the necessary steps to make your event a winner. It provides the particulars that make up the big picture of event planning, giving you advice, opinions, suggestions, tried-and-true methods, hints, tips, instructions and organizational plans. It will take you from the conceptual stage to writing thank you notes.

There is always something new or different that can enhance the logistics and creativity of planning an event. Things are changing all the time, whether it is new technology, new ways to "green" your event, new Internet services and applications, new or remodeled venues, contracts, or insurance laws. It is wise to keep up with new developments in all of these areas. Since my first edition in 2007, social media and new technology have exploded! Even the second edition in 2011 showed old Internet-related material. It changes so quickly — be sure to stay on top of the trends.

Even if you have been directing events for a long time, this book may teach you a new thing or two. Constant and continuing education is a common sense necessity in today's ever-changing landscape. I continue to learn and update my knowledge on the hospitality industry all the time.

For those of you new to event planning, this book will guide your progress, help organize your time, provide you with resources and suggestions to keep you focused, and allow you to look as though you have been an event planner for years. Best of all, it may keep you from making the costly and time-consuming mistakes thousands of planners have made before you. Just one or two of the tips suggested in this book can save you a great deal of money on one event alone and possibly save your job as well! Just read, follow, listen, learn and be flexible. One of the most important characteristics of an event planner is flexibility.

The Scope of This Book

The information in this guide is applicable to all events, whether it is the Academy Awards, Uncle Steve's 60th birthday party, the San Francisco Bay to Breakers run, the Sierra Club's annual conference for 2,000, or Googles' annual sales meeting. Each event has distinct characteristics, but they all have common threads weaving in and out of the planning process. These universal threads are only one aspect of what this guide presents. We will introduce and lead you through step-by-step details essential to designing and producing successful, memorable and extraordinary events. We will help you make smart decisions during the entire process so that you do not have to reinvent the wheel.

We cannot cover everything you need to know about event planning or prepare you for all the surprises, but we do offer the groundwork and a solid base of helpful information. It is your job to build on this foundation. Basic materials, tools and the draft schematics are provided; you bring in the subcontractors, work with the players, create the timelines, create and maintain the budget, and execute the details.

How and When to Use This Guide

There are several ways to get the most out of this guide. Read it from cover to cover, or go directly to a section relevant to your current circumstance. Wherever you are in the process, from the creation stage to deep into the details, you can find help in this book. Use it wisely and often. Keep it handy for reference, ideas and suggestions.

Although the sections are in sequence, they may not necessarily follow the flow or pertain to the decisions and strategies for your specific event. **Event planning is not a linear process.** One action does not necessarily or logically come after another. Some decisions are made simultaneously, while some must be subsequent to others. The process is different with each individual event. As you go through this guide and begin coordinating your event, you will understand. For instance, you cannot create the marketing material and begin your promotional efforts before you know where the event will be held. You need to know the dates and times before you select a site. You cannot invite the keynote speaker or book the entertainment until the goals, objectives and purpose for the event have been established. Even though events may not follow a defined sequence, the planning process can be simplified and organized if the guidelines and suggestions in this book are followed and close attention is paid to each step along the way.

There is some repetition of the content in the sections and chapters that is unavoidable. Planning involves activities that are interrelated. Consequently, each chapter, while integral to the whole, is also an independent component.

Benefits to the Reader

- Save time and money
- Develop your organizational skills
- Eliminate the guesswork
- Enhance your wealth of knowledge
- Answer common questions with tried-and-true solutions
- Offer ideas and suggestions
- Help you work within the constraints of time, materials and money
- Provide dozens of resources
- Define roles and responsibilities
- Present options to accomplish many tasks
- Help you make intelligent decisions
- Teach you money-saving techniques
- Make you efficient and competent
- Provide skillful negotiating techniques
- Show you how to wear many hats and juggle simultaneous tasks
- Make your efforts timely and systematic
- Relieve frustration
- Prepare you for the unexpected

Intended Audience

Anyone who is planning an event will benefit from this guide! It is chock full of solutions and experience, whether you are an administrative assistant, CEO, executive secretary, professional business person, manager, business owner, travel coordinator, an independent meeting planner, or just starting out in the meeting planning industry.

Whatever you do, wherever you work, reading this book will be worth your time. You have the valuable experience, great skills and natural talent required to become a great planner! We intend to enhance what you know and channel those talents into creating gratifying and rewarding events.

Too often the task of coordinating an event is given to the inexperienced, over-worked employee. Maybe you have been assigned, hired, asked to coordinate, or have made the choice to put on an event. The event may be job-related or a volunteer commitment with an association, an organization, a church, or social event. It might be your daughter's wedding or your partner's surprise 50th birthday party. It could be a four-day conference for 2,500 or an after-noon workshop for 20. It does not matter why you are doing it, what you are doing, or for whom you are doing it,, you will soon become the definitive multi-tasking planner.

Using Checklists and Timelines

Sample checklists and timelines located in the Appendix and on the companion CD-ROM serve as important planning tools in nearly every step in the process. They are extremely helpful in keeping you focused and on track. They are samples only, and you are encouraged to edit them to your specific needs since not all tasks will be appropriate for your specific event.

Checklists guarantee that significant and essential tasks and details are dealt with in a timely manner. Think of the checklist as an opportunity to double check everything, leaving all questions answered and tasks completed. When the tasks and details on the sample checklists are not appropriate to your event, tailor them to fit your own needs and goals.

Timelines will become your best friend if you use them. They are reminders for what needs to be done and when to do it. The complexity or simplicity of your timeline will be determined by the size and length of your event and, of course, your personality type.

Use these for yourself, with your staff, committees, vendors and suppliers, and anyone else involved in the process. They are useful in your meetings for delegating responsibilities, working with vendors, and designing and publishing marketing material. They are also useful when writing the summary report at the end of the event. Good lists with notations and dates are very useful in summing up the event when it is over.

What Should We Call It?

Since the word "event" is a general term used for hundreds of types of gatherings, it is difficult to focus on one or two specific types. So, in this book we speak about all events because they have a common element: a gathering of people for a specific purpose at a particular location.

The following chapter will help put into perspective the differences between business meetings/educational events and social/special events.

The job titles — coordinator, planner, producer, manager, director — are all used interchangeably. They all mean the person in charge of the day-to-day, hands-on business of planning the event — the one who makes it happen! The same goes for actions such as coordinating, planning and producing: They mean the act of doing your job. For the people participating in your event, we use a variety of words, such as guest, participant, attendee, member, ticket holder, employee, or audience.

Stories and Personal Experiences

Many of the stories come from my own and my colleagues' experiences. They show how a quick response can save an event. Often when something unplanned arises and the planner scrambles for the "fix," participants are unaware of any near-disaster. That is the sign of a great planner. These stories are true. Some of the names have been omitted to protect the innocent and the embarrassed (especially me). You can learn from our mishaps and on-the-run solutions and perhaps get a chuckle or two.

MONEY SAVING TIPS

Where appropriate, chapters will include money saving tips. They are only suggestions, but know that they have worked. Do not be afraid to ask for discounts, freebies, or extras. All experienced planners do. You will be amazed at what you can get with a smile and a courteous request.

Book Disclaimer

Event planning encompasses an enormous amount of information, and every event will have its own unique set of circumstances. We offer you the fundamentals in this book and suggest that you continue to learn by checking the resources listed in the back of this book and participating in continuing education.

My wish for you is that your events are successful, your goals and objectives are met, and you achieve a win-win situation for all concerned. Remember, enjoy yourself, keep smiling, and have fun!

The Anatomy of an Event

Coming together for a common purpose changes how we feel. It creates an environment that envelops the participants and influences them consciously and subconsciously. Even with today's sophisticated technology, there is no a substitute for the magic that occurs when people get together in one space for a common purpose. Being together in one space allows for teamwork, sharing, learning, fun, and networking that cannot be duplicated any other way. Magic truly does happen when we gather together with common goals.

The word event denotes an occasion, a gathering of people at a certain place at a certain time for a specific reason. Each occasion will have a unique name and purpose, but we will use the word event regularly and other synonyms as appropriate throughout this book. The names may be different, but the planning process remains the same.

The differences between each individual event might be:

- The reason your participants come together
- Who your attendees are
- The type of event organized

- The location
- Your planned goals and objectives

We gather people for a common purpose that is planned, organized, detailed and specific. You can successfully use the techniques in this book regardless of what you call it, where you hold it, or how many participants you have, etc. The importance lies in the similarities of events and using your skills, talents and experience to produce and manage them successfully.

Events often combine social, business and educational aspects, but most fall into one of these two groups.

Special and Social Events

Special events are the largest and broadest category of events. They can be open to the public at large with no admission requirements or specify a target audience with a registration fee. The size, shape and purpose of a special or social event are as assorted as the venues they are held in. They can include the Presidential Inauguration in the nation's capital, or a clambake at the local yacht club; the LPGA Tournament, a high school fundraiser for new band uniforms; a Farm Aid concert, or Billy and Sierra's science fair. The examples that follow are a partial list of special and social events:

- Anniversaries
- Art exhibits
- Auctions
- Award banquets
- Book signings
- Ceremonies
- Cocktail receptions

- Community programs
- Concerts
- Expositions
- Fairs
- Fashion shows
- Festivals
- Fundraisers

- Historic reenactments
- Galas
- Golf tournaments
- Parades
- Political rallies
- Reunions
- Road shows

- School functions
- Showers
- Sporting events
- Trade shows
- Tributes
- Weddings

Business and Educational Events

These events are typically corporate-, industry-, or education-related and are geared toward like-minded, work-oriented people. Usually they are specifically designed for a type of industry, certain topics, particular businesses, or training. They are rarely open to the public, but rather are reserved for peers, clients, students, customers, tradespeople, and associated industry or businesses and often have an educational element.

These types of events are usually organized within the corporation, association, or organization. Business and educational events include but are not limited to:

- Board meetings
- Classes
- Clinics
- Conferences
- Conventions
- Forums
- Intensives
- Lectures
- Meetings

- Retreats
- Sales meetings
- Seminars
- Sessions
- Shareholder meetings
- Symposiums
- Trainings
- Workshops

Why People Meet

The reasons people gather for events are as diverse as the people who attend them. You want to inspire, motivate, encourage, promote and entice people to come and participate. These reasons include one or usually more of the following:

- Annual meetings
- Appreciation dinners
- Attract new sponsors
- Boost morale
- Celebrations
- Communicate issues
- Education
- Entertainment/Fun
- Exchange ideas
- Force of habit
- Gain knowledge
- Get licensed
- Improve skills
- Increase membership
- Increase sales
- Job requirement
- Just because
- Make decisions
- Celebrate milestones
- Network
- Personal growth
- Play
- Promote a new product
- Public relations
- Raise money
- Recognition
- Solve problems
- Support a cause
- Training

Who Are Your Participants?

Whatever type of event you plan, it is for your participants. Who are they? Identifying and reaching the right people or group is crucial.

When targeting people in a specific profession, age group, or gender, finding your participants is straightforward. But if they are from a variety of groups or different areas, research may be necessary to find them.

People who attend events are members of associations, people with shared interests, or share common cause. They are members of professional organizations, social clubs, fellow sports enthusiasts, members of special interest groups, bridge club, yacht club, or family members to name a few.

If your goal is large attendance, finding your potential audience will require compiling mailing lists from many different sources and using multiple media efforts to get them to your event.

Doing some extensive research is recommended if you are questioning who your target market might be. You may want to survey potential attendees for insight into their needs, wants and requirements. After all, they will know what is current in their field and what is important to know. If it is an annual event, use past participants to gather the data. Although most answers come from planning sessions, send out a survey to a portion of your database. Here are a few possibilities of who they might be:

- Association members
- General public
- Like-minded people
- Women/Men/Both
- Specific age group
- Certain income bracket
- Similar ethnic backgrounds
- Religious or spiritual groups
- Technical or business related
- Family members
- Fellow workers
- Church group
- Similar interests and hobbies
- Groups with the same political views

Your target audience may be your company's employees. However, there may be dozens of departments and different levels of management that are part of your target. Even though you know exactly where they are, you will still need to do some research to reach them.

If you are planning an all-day seminar for meeting planners, where will these participants come from? You can buy a list, create them from contacts and networking, or advertise for them. Do your research. Once you know who and where they are, attracting them is the next step.

If your event is a brand new art and music festival, will the town members be enough to make your event successful, or will you have to go to the surrounding towns and market there? How far will you have to go to attract like-minded people to your event and get enough people to meet your financial goal? These are questions that will be answered in your planning sessions.

Location, Location, Location

As in business and real estate, location is a key factor in the success of an event. You want to match the location to the style of your event, your audience, your theme and your purpose. The location should fit the occasion and be accessible for the majority of your guests. Remember, you are not limited to the standard locations such as hotels, convention centers, or restaurants.

Here is a partial list of meeting places. ***Do not limit your imagination; be creative!***

- Airport hotels
- Airport hangars
- Amusement parks
- Aquariums
- Arenas
- Armories

- Art galleries
- Atriums
- Backyards
- Beaches
- Boat charters
- Churches/Chapels/ Synagogues/Temples
- Coliseums
- Colleges/Universities
- Community centers
- Conference centers
- Cruise ships
- Downtown hotels
- Downtown streets/square
- Dude ranches
- Fairgrounds
- Gardens
- Golf or country clubs
- Libraries
- Mansions
- Mountain tops
- Museums
- Parks/Campgrounds
- Parking lots
- Race tracks
- Resorts
- Restaurants
- Retreat centers
- Skating rinks
- Ski resorts
- Sports facilities
- Tennis courts
- Art theaters
- Town halls
- Warehouses
- Wineries
- Yachts or yacht club
- Zoos

What All Events Have in Common

These are the five areas of event planning that are found in every event, regardless of the size, place, date, reason, etc. Each of these areas will be addressed in the upcoming sections.

Goals and objectives

Every event will have goals and objectives, whether they are set, discussed and confirmed upfront or not. What is your purpose for having the event?

Date, time and site selection

When and where combined with location equals the foundation of an event! Every event needs a site! It might be your backyard, PacBell Park, Grace Cathedral or downtown San Francisco and Golden Gate Park. It could be your local town hall, social club building, or a mansion on Nob Hill. But it will be somewhere!

Promotion and marketing

You must get the message out. The message could be as simple as the date, time, location and reason via the telephone for a surprise birthday party. It could be as complicated as material for a week-long convention with numerous workshops, special events, outside excursions, banquets and required registration information. Delivering this amount of information can take a multipage brochure. It may require a quarter-page ad in your local newspaper or a full-page ad in *The New York Times*. The larger the event, the more likely you will need to make a website and engage in social media and social networking.

Participants/attendees

Without people, you would not have an event. Everyone needs participants to have an event. Whether they are invited guests, paying participants, or required attendees, people will be coming to your event.

Agenda

This is what is happening from before the participants arrive to the follow-up when the event is complete. This is a detailed outline of the activities of the event. The agenda tells people where to go, what to do when they get there, etc. The agenda can one of be two types. One type is for the participants. They receive it and follow the scheduled events. The other type of agenda is for the people working the event to follow. Some events will have both types of agendas.

Job of an Event Planner

Event planning is a process that starts by delineating the beginning and the end of the event. At that point, it becomes a project, and you are the project manager! It is not like your typical job where you go in and do the same thing every day. Your tasks and responsibilities change each day during the process and will be different with each event.

The job of the planner varies according to the size, scope and complexity of the event. You may be asked to do any number of different tasks, including but not limited to client consultation, setting budgets, choosing dates, selecting and inspecting a location, negotiating with and choosing suppliers, arranging transportation, booking blocks of hotel rooms, arranging catering, booking entertainment or speakers, writing copy for publicity, gathering leads for potential participants, choosing printers, creating agendas, hiring security, writing an environmental checklist, signing contracts, dealing with lawyers, compiling participants' packets, gathering and directing volunteers, sticking on labels, or shipping boxes. And that is all before the event even begins.

Each event is complex and diverse with unique characteristics. There can be thousands of details associated with one event. You will wear many hats, juggle a number of tasks simultaneously and use many skills. One day you may be talking with a hotel and negotiating room rates, the next you are working on the budget, and later that afternoon you are writing copy for your website. You may be entering names into a database one day and stuffing envelopes or flying off to do a site inspection the next. You will be interacting with chief executive officers, talent agents, general managers, waiters, house cleaners, and everyone in-between. You will meet and talk to different people every day.

The Big Picture

Defining Your Purpose

Being focused from the beginning is essential. This is the time to define what your purpose is, what you want to achieve and to commit those intentions to paper. Do this by defining your goals and objectives, setting your financial goals, identifying your participants, and creating environmental standards and corporate social responsibilities. Begin to envision how the event will look and feel. These decisions and positions form the framework of the event and will be fleshed out right to the end.

Your defined purpose outlines everything that you do from this point forward. All the marketing material, each agenda, your choice of speakers or entertainment, the location and much more will be based on and related to this purpose. In this section, we begin the developing stages and help you clearly define your purpose and weave it into the final product.

The most efficient and effective way to create your purpose is to hold a planning session with your staff or client and begin generating attainable goals and measurable objectives. After the purpose is determined, you can create committees and assign roles, responsibilities, and tasks. At this point, you can establish whether you need to hire outside consultants, vendors, and suppliers during these sessions. Outsourcing some responsibilities and tasks may be necessary to save you time and money.

During this meeting or at subsequent meetings, develop financial goals. Is the event a for-profit event, and if so, how much will we need to charge? If it is not for-profit, how will we measure our return on investment? You need to know what your break-even point is and how to go about attaining it. If it is not-for-profit, pinpoint the source of the money. These questions and more will be determined in your planning sessions. See more about financial goals in Chapter 6?

We recommend that you create timelines and checklists and amend them during and after planning sessions. The *Appendix* and the companion CD-ROM have samples of these forms for most areas of the planning process. Use these important tools to help remember the smallest details. Sometimes the smallest details can make or break an event.

Time spent in planning, writing and designing your event in the early stages will result in increased attendance, repeat business, more publicity and more money (or all the above, or whatever your goals and objectives are).

No event is too small for an official planning session. Even if there are only two people attending the meeting, you still need to cover all of the basics: who, what, when, where, and why. No event is planned without answering those questions.

Goals and Objectives

Each event should have a goal and an objective that form the purpose of your event. Without them, you have no defined purpose and no direction. We define goals and objectives as follows:

Goal – The general purpose of the event that provides a road map for the planning process.

Objective – A measurable, attainable target that contributes to the accomplishment of the goal.

An event can have one or many goals and typically multiple objectives supporting the goals. Call them what you like, but setting goals and objectives is necessary for a successful event.

Companies, organizations, promoters, associations, charities and people in general produce events for many reasons. There should be more than one purpose for your event. For example, you may want education to be the defined purpose, but you would also like to raise money, gain publicity and have fun as well.

The partial list below shows examples of potential goals and objectives. Your participants often want or require one or more reasons to come to your event.

Possible goals and objectives

- Accreditation /Certification
- Attract members
- Celebrate
- Charity
- Come to a decision
- Community relations
- Conduct business
- Develop

- Display
- Educate
- Gain knowledge
- Entertain
- Explore
- Gain publicity
- Have fun
- Improve skills
- Incentive enhancing
- Inform
- Inspire
- Introduce likeminded people
- Introduce new officers or board members
- Introduce new product or policy
- Improvement
- Learn something new
- Make a profit
- Motivate
- Network
- Professional advancement
- Recreation
- Reward
- Save the environment
- Share and exchange information
- Solve problems
- Support
- Train

Financial Goals

Financial goals reflect your defined purpose and the decisions you make regarding the return on your investment. Establish your financial goals before creating your budget. It is similar to defining your goals and objectives before defining the type of event to produce.

Financial goals should fit into your overall goals and objectives. Your goal may be goodwill, promotion of a product or something that will not have a monetary bottom line. However, a great number of events are produced for the sole purpose of making money. It is recommended that you set your financial goals early in the planning stages if profit is your purpose. With financial goals set, you can create your budget, price the registration/ticket fee, choose the location and make important decisions on the costly aspects.

Return on investment (ROI)

There are many ways to evaluate and measure the return on investment (ROI). It is not just about money. Your objective may be profit, goodwill or a testament of gratitude! It might have to do with the future of your business by training your sales team on new techniques or increasing productivity by introducing new technology, creating spiritual seminars, going on tour to sell more music CDs and merchandise, raising money for a good cause or giving motivational incentives. Whatever the financial goals or objectives are, they must have significance and be part of your defined purpose. If it is profit that you are after, your ROI is calculated by simply dividing your net profit by your total costs, and the result is the percentage of financial gain. Each and every event will have its unique return on investment.

When it is profit you want, establish a solid budget, and implement a measuring tool that will meet your objectives. If a sales increase is your goal, your annual sales report would be your measuring tool. If new members are your goal, then your membership records would be your tool.

Internal ROI

If it is goodwill you seek or the demonstration of thanks, you have to use other measures of success. They may be seeing the large smile of the corporate executive as you present him or her a fabulous parting gift, witnessing the excitement of new members as they join the organization, earning recognition for a job well done, honoring the top sales force with incentive travel packages, getting publicity in the local newspaper, engaging a town with a local festival or simply honoring a long-time employee.

External ROI

The ROI can be aimed at your participants, guests and attendees. When that is the case, measuring success is difficult. You can collect information through evaluation forms, receipt of thank you notes an increase in enrollment, higher donations, more volunteers or the bottom line.

Regardless of what your ROI is all about, it must be important to you and your organization, your clients and sales force, your family or peers, your city or town, or whoever is the beneficiary of the event.

The Planning Sessions

We cannot emphasize enough the importance of the planning sessions. These sessions furnish insight in making all of your future decisions with purpose and intention. You will set goals and objectives, begin designing your event, establish roles and responsibilities, identify and understand your target audience, as well as set dates, times, locations and themes. This process might be frustrating at times, but if you get it right from the start, you will benefit by enjoying a smooth, well-run event with great results.

The decisions made in this meeting will be created, refined, confirmed and even transformed with time. These sessions will set the stage and create the foundation of the event. Use this time to establish the key decision makers, core planners and internal resources as well as to decide whether outside help is necessary.

Planning sessions should include all the significant players — those people who will be involved in the entire process: your staff, hired consultants, vendors, accounting department, etc. Working together, all interested parties can arrive at a better understanding of how the event fits into the goals and objectives of the organization planning the event. If they cannot attend the planning session, make sure they get the notes and summary report. If there is more than one meeting, continue to pass on the notes and reports.

These pre-event meetings are critical for the success of your event and will help to alleviate misunderstandings, create a cooperative atmosphere and proceed with focus and clarity.

When each meeting concludes, write a summary of the decisions and distribute it to the appropriate people for those who did not attend. This allows them to pick up the file and carry on the process if for some reason, you — the planner — have to drop out.

If this is a repeat event, go over the final report from past events including the participants' evaluation summaries and the event planners' notes with improvement strategies. These historical notes are golden and will save you time, frustration and money. Do not try to reinvent the wheel, but be sure to improve upon and even make some drastic changes if necessary, especially if the old ways are obsolete. For some events with a long history, it will be a challenge to blend tradition and innovation. It will be your job to keep the tradition of the event while also being relevant and contemporary.

A full day of initial planning is suggested for larger events, preferably two days if time allows, or they can be broken into smaller meetings over many days. Have these meetings periodically to report status and changes. It might be a good idea to have a "management retreat" at the same time as an intensive decision-making meeting. This is a critical time for discovering what you have to offer and deciding what outside help is needed to put on an extraordinary show!

Designing the Planning Session

Decide the framework for generating your first planning session(s). Answer these questions and add to the specifications as needed.

- Who should attend?
- Who will run the meeting?
- How many meetings are needed?
- How long for each meeting?
- Who will create the agenda?
- What goals and objectives will be discussed and determined?
- Who, what, when, where and why—logistics?
- Who gets the summary, reports and notes?
- Where will the meeting be held? What do you do first?

TIPS

Everyone involved in the event must communicate regularly: That means having meetings. Nine or 10 months out, a monthly meeting is fine, but as the big date approaches, go to bi-weekly or weekly meetings to make sure no one drops the ball and everyone has up-to-date information. It is vital that good notes be taken at these meetings. People may forget what they volunteered for, dates might be confused, and the minutes may end up being a real lifesaver. If these records or minutes are lengthy, do not waste time reading them at each meeting. Get them copied and emailed out in advance of the meeting, and ask for any corrections before meeting time excluding typos and spelling errors.

Think big picture. What goals do you want to achieve? They should be strategic in nature, setting the stage for creating objectives to support them. If the question is, why have the event in the first place, the answer is in your goals. Bring the following questions to the meeting to get your creative juices flowing for consideration on your goals and objectives.

High level – goal questions

- What is your event's primary emphasis, the overall purpose? Is it educational, fun, a product release, fundraising, an anniversary celebration or to make money?
- Will this event be for the audience or for the organization? Who is the beneficiary?
- How important is financial success? Is our main focus profit, benevolence or public relations?
- What information will you be sharing? Will it introduce something new: a sales strategy, product line, CD or fundraising strategy?
- What location is best? Where are most of your participants located? Will they travel, do we need a popular destination, and is money an issue for those coming?
- What is the target date? Is it determined by the month, season, year or day of week?
- Who is your target audience? Are they our employees, family, club members, sales team, like-minded people, industry groups or students?
- Why do they want to attend? Is it education, fun, entertainment, interest or a job requirement?
- Is the event required attendance, or will they be paying?
- Can they afford to attend? Who will pay for their registration, travel, lodging and other expenses?

- What is your budget? Is this a rate-conscious group? Are we making a profit?

- What kind of space is required? Is it luxury, business, economy, fun or adventure?

- Will we need sponsors? Do we need to find additional funding?

- Is this a repeat event? If so, what were the results of the last event? Is there past data? What do we need to do differently?

- Are your participants repeats? Did they attend your past events? What evaluations were received?

- Is networking an important component?

- Are exhibits a component, either as a source of revenue or information?

- Will there be off-site events?

- How does environmental planning contribute to all of our decisions?

- What corporate social responsibilities (CSRs) will we establish?

- Do we have environmental standards, or do we need to establish some?

Below are a few samples of measurable objectives. Often more than one objective will be appropriate for each event.

- Increase sales by 20 percent.
- Teach participants about a new product.
- Provide training to sales staff.
- Define roles and responsibilities for the new planning committee.
- Roll out a new marketing program.
- Bring the family together for a celebration.
- Recruit 50 new members.
- Network with five new companies in similar business.
- Introduce 50,000 people to new software.
- Sell 500 "how-to" tapes, and teach 1,000 people how to buy real estate.

- Earn a profit of $75,000.

- Sell 20,000 CDs and other merchandise.

- Introduce new board of directors.

- Raise money for political candidate.

- Announce new product to public.

- Celebrate partner Sande's birthday.

TIPS

➥ Have a good established agenda for planning session. Do not waste people's valuable time.

➥ Have available past documentation that will be used and discussed.

➥ Have a complete agenda prepared.

➥ Use local hotel space for your meeting if off-site is necessary.

Timing is Everything

Give yourself plenty of time for planning every aspect of the event. You will be surprised how much time certain tasks require be it designing, writing, and editing marketing material, creating lists, mailing, finding the right caterer or choosing a menu. For instance, venues typically need to be booked years ahead of time and really popular or well-known speakers and entertainers fill their calendars months or years in advance.

Sometimes you can pull off a large event in a short time, but there is usually a price to pay—and not just money. You may not get the venue you want, the participants you need or the right speaker or entertainer. You may have to take second-best or end up using leftovers. It is best to give yourself plenty of buffer time. It is far easier to be early in planning than too late. One of the biggest reasons for a failed event is misjudging the timing.

Assigning Roles and Responsibilities

Assign roles and responsibilities early in the process. There are many areas to cover, details to attend to, decisions to be made, and someone needs to be in charge. Who?

You may be a one-person show with all the decision-making power, if you are putting on a one-day workshop for yourself. You are it! Or you could work for a large corporation like Costco where you are one of many planners and decision makers. You may be the event planner for a resort, in which case the boss is the final decision maker, but you are also a decision maker in some areas. The scenarios are endless. This will also allow you to recognize when outsourcing (using outside vendors) is necessary.

You may be the chief, but if you are part of a larger corporation or association or one of several people working together, breaking up the duties can be extremely helpful. If the event is large, you might want to break down the roles and responsibilities in the following manner. This breakdown can be useful also when the event is smaller to keep your staff from getting in each other's way. Make descriptions of each position and the responsibilities that can be used year after year. Key areas/teams at a very high level: Remember, you may be a one-person team.

- **Operational** – This team has the overall responsibility of operations of the event, including management of all team members.

- **Financial** – This team determines sources of revenue, creates budgets and financial timelines, and designs the accounting systems.

- **Marketing** – This team knows the audience, promotional techniques, how to reach participants, how to design and implement the process, and understands the latest technology strategies.

- **Legal** – This team is clear on contracts, insurance, taxes and is skilled at negotiations.

- **Program** – This team designs what happens from the moment the event begins to the moment it ends and they will choose entertainment, speakers, session subjects, etc. You may want to break up into smaller committees such as activities, vendors, auction, etc.

Roles and responsibilities will vary depending on the variables of your event. There are thousands of little jobs. Who is going to do them? Some tasks can be assigned right away and others can be assigned as coordination moves forward. You may be responsible for logistics while others are responsible for writing and designing marketing materials and someone else is responsible for creating the agenda and obtaining permits. Someone different may handle financial tasks. Be clear about who is doing what. Most importantly, know who can make financial decisions and who has the last say.

Here are some questions, suggestions and issues to be discussed:

- Who is the head coordinator?
- Determine decision-making chain of command.
- How many committees are needed?
- Who is in charge of each committee?
- How often should the committees meet?

- Divide areas of responsibility: program committee, operations, logistics, budgeting and promotions.
- Create checklists with appropriate details.
- Create schedules with achievable dates.
- After a committee's job is complete, place the members on another committee.
- Assign specific tasks to those responsible. When setting up committees, try to match skills and talents with responsibilities.

TIPS ON MAINTAINING SUCCESS

Should your event be so successful that it becomes an annual thing, congratulations! Now you have another potential problem: burnout! If the same person is in charge of the same portion of the event for three years in a row, I suggest that an assistant be assigned so that she or he can take over the job the following year. This is important because 1) it will take some of the load off the veteran and 2) it is a perfect training opportunity for the future planner to get him or her up to speed before taking over.

Some people are too proud to accept help, thinking that it makes them look incompetent. This way they will get assistance automatically, without feeling inadequate. If your event is really successful, they will need all the help they can get anyway.

Creating Timelines and Checklists

Do not underestimate the value of timelines and checklists. Just like every component in the process, timelines and checklists will vary depending on your unique circumstances. These tools keep everyone involved on track and help you meet your deadlines! If you want to meet your deadlines, refine your timelines and checklists, and use them often! See the sample checklists and timelines in the *Appendix* Section. Amend these samples to reflect your specific event.

Timelines

Timelines are used to meet critical dates. You can create your timelines with key dates or milestones only, or you can be incredibly detailed with each task and deadline listed. It is your choice. Use the timeline that works best according to your event. We suggest creating several timelines for different areas of responsibility.

A detailed timeline will ensure that no task or detail goes undone. Take these questions into consideration when creating your timeline:

- Who is it for? The planner, the staff, the committees or all of these.
- Who should create them?
- How many are needed?
- Who is the keeper?
- How often will they be revised? Daily, weekly, monthly.
- Should you use software application to help manage?
- When to begin creating the timeline?
- Are the dates attainable and reasonable?

The best time to create a timeline is either during or after the planning session, after the dates are confirmed, after your site has been confirmed or whenever you see appropriate. Remember the purpose of the timeline is to keep you on track. Therefore, start early, and keep it amended! One way to create a timeline is to start from the day of the event and work backward. It may seem strange at first, but it works! Remember, revise your timeline as often as needed. The point is to get everything down and give you enough time to complete each task.

Checklists

Similar to the timeline, checklists will vary depending on circumstances. They will keep you and everyone else moving steadily without omitting any details. The smallest missed task can ruin your day and throw off your schedule. If a task is written down, the chances of doing that task increases dramatically. Get it down on paper.

When is the best time to create checklists? Create checklists during or after the planning session, after dates are confirmed, when roles and responsibilities have been defined or whenever it is appropriate for you. The purpose of the checklist is to organize all the details. Be smart, and start early!

As you develop your checklist, include as much detail as possible for each task. For example, for the "day of the event" checklist, assign these types of tasks:

- Set up briefing with volunteers and staff
- Arrange for airport pickup for VIPs, speakers and entertainment
- Assign supervisor for A-V equipment
- Find greeter
- Find Help Desk personnel

- Assign supervisor for breaks
- Assign supervisor for meeting room set-up
- Hang signs
- Meet with facility personnel
- Make sure to have cash on hand
- Have revised participants list

Refer to and use the sample timelines and checklists in the *Appendix.*

Edit them to fit your particular circumstances. We expect that you will build upon them since they are samples only and will not cover all the details for your event.

Outsourcing

Outsourcing is hiring professionals outside your company who are experts in a particular field to do a specific job or task. These professionals can be from a variety of businesses, including a temp service to staff your registration table, a florist to decorate your space, a security or audiovisual specialist, vendors and suppliers of all kinds, marketers, designers, tradespeople and consultants. In the planning sessions, decide whether you need outside help and can afford it. Seasoned planners know when to use outside professional services for a variety of jobs.

Outsourcing can save time, money and frustration. Consider hiring an expert to do the task if there is funding for outside help whenever a job is outside of your skills or experience or you lack personnel or time. Even hiring an independent meeting planner can save you money. When you decide to use outside assistance, create a partnership with the person or firm. Share the re-sponsibility, and commit to open and continuing communication. Pass on the most descriptive and detailed job description that you can to attract the most qualified person or firm. Bidders will want to know what their responsibilities will be from the beginning. Of course, their duties may change slightly as the event begins to draw nearer.

Pick someone who can grasp your purpose and agrees with the culture of your business and the level of service you expect them to provide. Succinct directions are important to this person. You may want to create a request for proposal (RFP) when searching for this person.

Examples of services you may need to outsource:

- Advertising/Publicity/Public relations
- Airline and travel agencies
- Audiovisual technology companies
- Balloon makers
- Caterers
- Convention and Visitors Bureau (CVB)
- Copying services/Printing
- Destination Management Company (DMC)
- Entertainment/Staging company
- Equipment rental
- Florists/Decorations
- Graphic designer
- Ground transportation
- Hospitality greeters
- Interpreters
- Linens
- Mailing house
- Marketing
- Meeting facility
- Publishing
- Registration company
- Security companies
- Speakers bureaus
- Trades people
- Travel directories
- Temporary workers
- Tent rentals
- Web designers

For outdoor events, several services and vendors must be put under contract: a hotdog vendor, cotton candy and snow cone maker for a fair or party; a caterer, a tent company, security team, buses and valet attendants for other types of events. Sporting events have dozens of vendors responsible for tasks such as parking, security, food, T-shirt sales or registrations. If possible, get references before hiring and signing any contracts. Use vendors who have a track record or who were recommended by someone you trust.

If your event is in a town other than where you live, contact the local convention and visitors bureau (CVB) or the local destination management companies (DMC), and communicate with other event planners in that area for suggestions and recommendations.

Where is the Money?

It is time to manifest the financial goals determined in the planning session. To initiate the financial process, begin by creating your budget. A budget is a written document forecasting the potential costs and income of the event. It is a great monitoring tool for your spending. A well-created and maintained budget is an essential tool to allow you to project and supervise income and expenses, track cash flow and verify how well you are doing at any given time. It will serve as your guide throughout the planning process. You will refer to it often and edit and update frequently.

The budget is incredibly important for many reasons. A realistic budget in the beginning will help determine whether to take on the event. It will facilitate the decision-making process from start to finish and is a critical tool to help you spend your money wisely. It will also create the numbers for the formulas needed to find your break-even point and return on investment.

To have an accurate budget, you must know the source, arrival date and amount of money that will be coming in. Identify your revenue and income so that you can plan when and how to spend it. Every expense goes into the budget. As you continue the process of planning your event and encounter more expenses, immediately put them into your budget.

Use historical data if available. Go over past budgets, and see where you can either tighten or expand your services. Take into consideration expense versus income, and determine whether your registration fee or ticket price was too inexpensive or too pricey for your intended audience. Compare what you projected as opposed to the actual expenses. Note the most significant miscalculations. If this is a first-time event, you can begin with a zero-based budget to be built on estimated expenditures and income.

Always take your defined purpose into consideration when creating line items for your budget. You may desire fine wines, exotic flowers, exquisite food and a venue with a breathtaking view but end up with taped music, simple decorations and paper plates because you run out of money. You decide where to spend your money. If your defined purpose is to honor and impress the new board of directors, you will fail with paper plates. Your budget will keep you from making mistakes in spending and instead assist you in making educated decisions.

Determine early on where the money will be coming from and how much you will need. There are four sources of the money: your own reserves, sponsorship, participants or a combination. Sponsors may make product donations that will offset your cash outflow. If the source is your participants, take into consideration that a large percentage of the money will be spent before money will be coming back your way.

When expenses and income have been placed in the budget, find your break-even point, and determine what style of accounting is appropriate for your event.

Creating a Budget

As you begin to plan your event, laying out your proposed budget on a cost sheet will allow you to see what items can be included while staying within your budget. Watching the spending activity gives you the opportunity to use alternative options if the budget becomes overextended. Should you find extra money, you may be able to add frills to the event or find a large profit coming your way. Each event requires different expenditures so that there is no set formula or format for the budget. Walk through the event, and write down all costs, taking everything into consideration. Revise the numbers as you get estimates and actual costs. Suppliers are happy to furnish you with written estimates for many of the expensive items your event will require. Get as many estimates as you can while you build your budget. The more accurate the numbers are in the beginning, the better the bottom line will be at the end. You can have a wish list of items for the event if money is available.

Revenue/income stream

Revenue can come to you in a variety of ways: contributions, registration fees, sponsorship, sales (T-shirts, books, audio tapes or advertising space), franchise fees, exhibit space or ticket sales. If you have a private individual writing a check to cover costs, consider yourself lucky. Not every event will generate income, but there must be a revenue stream or a source of money to pay the bills.

Using sponsorship

Sponsorship is a common and widespread method used to help fund an event. It is a great way to create a relationship or partnership with an organization or company that can last for years. It is a win-win situation for all concerned. The company gets name recognition and a direct line to their market base.

The event gets extra money, products or donations to defray out-of-pocket costs, either in the form of cash or in-kind contributions (products). The participant gets information, product usage, information about the company and its products and perhaps free gifts or product samples.

Companies no longer just sponsor an event for charity. Charitable intent might be part of the reason, but there are other motives behind sponsorship. Companies use these events as marketing vehicles to help them reach their customers. The days of sponsors writing large checks, sending you their logos for promotional material, supplying products and then walking away are over. Promotional tie-ins pop up in almost every aspect of today's events.

Sponsorship is a direct way to build branding and product recognition to an audience, typically their customers, users, clients and purchasers. A potential sponsor will want to reach large numbers of customers at one time or a very specific group of people. They can be creative in their marketing efforts with their name on printed materials, signs, mementos and hands-on usage at the event. Participants associated with a specific event (charity, environmental, political, philosophic or cultural) can be allied with the product the sponsor wants to promote. When looking for a sponsor, take into consideration how the participants and the products will match and if one is appropriate for the other. When you do partner with a sponsor, remember to give them VIP treatment, and keep them in the loop as the event planning progresses.

Build a lasting relationship with that sponsor, but be careful to avoid a hard-sell approach towards your attendees. Do not force the sponsors' message, and ease up on the "we want to thank our sponsors" speeches.

Event: 10K Walk
Fundraiser
350 Participants
Downtown San Francisco

I was the coordinator in charge of promotion and marketing during one of my first sporting events. I had worked on several other events that had history and several solid sponsors. I was determined to find my own, and I did. Fortunately, many companies agreed that giving products was a great way to hit their target market. For one event, I was able to get fanny packs from a well-known sporting goods manufacturer, cases of a new soft drink that was being marketed, corn nuts, T-shirts with their logo and coupons for a trip to the spa. I was delighted as were the participants of the event. Although there was no hard cash involved, the donations saved thousands of dollars in out-of-pocket expenses, and the registrants walked away happy with all the products. The company that donated the soft drinks was so generous that we had twice the number of drinks as we had participants. We were able to save the remaining drinks for the following event.

Lesson Learned: Product sponsorship can be lucrative.

Shannon

Expenses

Expenses fall into three categories: fixed, indirect and variable costs. Almost any fixed cost can turn into a variable cost if the event or meeting grows significantly or if you provide additional services or attractions. Likewise, variable expenses can turn into fixed expenses. We have included an important list of expenses that many planners forget to figure into the budget. This list will help you create the most precise budget possible, but as always, something may slip through the cracks. Here is a brief description of the type of expenses you may encounter.

Fixed costs

Fixed expenses are unchangeable regardless of sales or profits and are not adjusted based on the number of participants. Often they cannot be changed even when revenue falls short of expectations. A partial list of typical fixed expenses:

Fixed expenses

- Audiovisual equipment
- Entertainment
- Insurance
- Marketing and promotion
- Meeting site/facility/venue

- Personnel salaries
- Signs
- Speakers
- Technology
- Transportation

Variable expenses

Variable expenses fluctuate based on the number of participants. You can calculate from the variable expenses just how much you will spend per person. A partial list of variable expenses:

Variable expenses

- Accommodations
- Additional site rental fees
- Communications costs
- Decorations
- Food and beverage
- Gifts

- Invitations/Registration forms/Brochures
- Labor charges
- Lighting
- Mailing
- Marketing and promotion

- Menus
- Nametags/Placards
- Office supplies
- Photography
- Placards
- Power charges
- Promotional material
- Rehearsal costs
- Security
- Shipping, handling and drayage
- Signs
- Special effects
- Staffing
- Staging
- Taxes
- Transportation
- Travel (to site inspection)
- Wages for temporary staff

Events not held in a contained facility such as a hotel, club, restaurant or convention center will require additional cost considerations. When the event is held outdoors in a park, at the fairgrounds, within the town plaza or at the botanical garden, plan for the costs of these services in your budget. Some items to consider:

Additional expenses – outside facility

- Alcohol sales/Liquor permit
- Catering
- Cancellation fees
- Glasses, dishes, silverware
- Insurance – both you and contractors
- Labor
- Parking
- Parking attendants
- Permits
- Power
- Security
- Signs
- Staff – maintenance, electrician, engineers, stagehands
- Staging equipment
- Tables and chairs
- Tablecloths/Skirting
- Tents
- Themes and decorations
- Toilets
- Traffic control
- Waste/Trash removal

The following is a list of expenses to be conscious about within a contained facility. Charges of this nature can be an unpleasant surprise on your final bill. Ask about these or other types of charges, fees or tips, and negotiate these costs before signing the contract.

Additional expenses – contained Facility

- Audiovisual setup
- Attrition
- Baggage handling
- Cleaning
- Computer
- Copying
- Early departure
- Easel rental
- Electricians, maintenance, engineers
- Energy surcharge
- Extension cord
- Fax sending and receiving
- Gratuity
- Hanging banners and signs
- Health club
- Hotel shuttle
- Internet access
- Meeting room setup
- Meeting room key
- Mini-bar usage
- Minimum bartender
- Loading dock access
- Parking
- Package delivery
- Per-person minimum
- Phone access
- Resort
- Room delivery
- Safety-deposit box
- Security
- Storage
- Taxes
- Technology

Discuss these fees and expenses with the venue to eliminate any surprise charges on the final bill.

Indirect costs

These costs are related to your organization's overhead. Administration costs, salaries and office equipment.

MONEY SAVING TIPS

➥ Get several bids for the major expenses and some of the smaller ones. You will be surprised at the amount of money you can save by comparing bids for products and services. When a vendor knows you are getting additional bids, their prices many come down.

➥ Create a simple spreadsheet with associated costs to calculate their impact on your meeting budget. If you are comparing two cities, a difference of a few percentage points in taxes can make a big difference in the cost of your event.

➥ Choose a city with low overall tax and travel tax bases.

➥ Are you tax exempt? Learn the rules for charities and non-profit companies. Can you be invoiced out-of-province or out-of-state and eliminate taxes? What are the rules for charging tax on gratuities or services? Are you eligible for tax breaks that you are not claiming? A good tax consultant can answer these questions.

➥ Calculate your fixed, variable and break-even costs. Know where your soft costs are and what is non-negotiable to your program so that you have an idea of where you could spend less or what can be eliminated completely.

➥ Budget a 10 percent contingency to take care of unforeseen costs (for example, strikes or bad weather).

➥ Use volunteers when possible, either from the community, your organization or club, or from a fan base.

Breaking even

If profit is your goal, you will need to know the break-even point. To get this measurement, a well-established budget is necessary. If your money is coming from registration, you need to know how many participants it takes to break even. If you know the number of participants, you will need to know how much to charge for registration or ticket sales.

How many participants are needed to break even?

Here is a sample calculation to find your break-even point. Add up your fixed costs and include site rental, speaker fees and expenses, and marketing costs. Let us use $75,000 fixed costs. Now add up your variable costs on a per person basis, including food and beverage, registration material and shipping. Let us use $200 per person cost. Using a registration fee of $500 per person, deduct the variable costs. Divide the remaining amount into the fixed costs. Therefore, you would need 250 participants to break even. We used the following formula: Fixed costs ÷ (Registration fee – Variable costs) = number of required participants.

$$\$75,000 \div (\$500 - \$200) = 250$$

How to set registration or ticket fees to break even

If you have a good idea of the number of attendees or participants anticipated, you can find your break-even point and set your fees accordingly. You need to have your fixed and variable costs calculated using the confirmed number of participants. Add these two costs together and divide that number by your projected attendance. For example, using 250 participants, $200 variable expense and total fixed expenses of $75,000, you would need to charge $500 to break even.

$$(\$75,000 + \$50,000) \div 250 \text{ participants} = \$500$$

Equipped with these numbers, you can determine whether you can make a profit. If the numbers do not work, here are some things you can do to change the financial dynamics:

- Increase attendance
- Increase registration fee
- Solicit sponsorship
- Reduce expenses

Accounting Styles

Your accounting style should be based on your knowledge of event costs, availability of software and the type of event you are producing. If your event is small, perhaps recording your expenses can be a matter of filing all of your receipts in a folder and entering numbers on an Excel spreadsheet. But the larger the event, the more important spending becomes, making proper recording practices a must.

When your profit is your goal, a more sophisticated system should be used. There are two popular accounting methods used in recording income and expenditures: cash accounting and accrual accounting.

Cash accounting is a simple and basic method and not really an up-to-date accounting of the big picture. It is basically recording your income and expenditures when they are received and when they are paid. Compare it to your checkbook record. When a deposit is made, it is added to the accounting record. When a receipt is paid, it is entered into the recording device. This does not take into consideration any outstanding and known expenses yet to be paid or any outstanding unpaid income, but it may suit the purpose for your event. Do not make it more difficult than need be.

The **accrual accounting** method is a little more complicated, but it is more accurate because it takes into consideration money that has yet to be spent or received. It accounts for committed income and expenses in the month that they are expected to be acquired or paid. In other words, accrual accounting shows money as income even though you have not received it and shows money debited even though it has not been paid out.

Keeping up with the spending activity is also very important for larger events. Review and update the accounting ledger and budget regularly during the course of the planning process.

Payment method options

If you will be collecting money for your event, here are some options to consider:

Cash or Check	Low tech and costs nothing but your time. Depending on the size of your event, processing checks and counting cash could be a minor annoyance or a major accounting nightmare. Depending on your audience and their adoption of other payment methods, you may have to allow for mail-in payments in one form or another.
Credit Cards	If you still rely on paper or faxed registration forms, your attendees can write in their credit card information, and you can punch their numbers into a Point-of-Sale (POS) machine. Some planners will even take credit card information over the phone. Although still a manual process, it's better than batching hundreds of checks for deposit. A few words of caution —be careful to destroy the full credit card number once you've processed the charge (keep the last four digits for reconciliation), and NEVER take credit card information over email.
Payment Service Providers	Payment service providers offer a secure channel for moving funds, some basic reporting and alerts for failed transactions, as well as the ability to issue refunds directly. Here are several of the most popular providers. Please do your own research to see which of these, if any, are right for your specific event. PayPal, Google Wallet, Amazon Payments, Dwolla, Authorize.net and others. As of this writing, PayPal is the most popular with Google Wallets gaining ground. Do your research.
Third Party	There are companies that will collect credit card payments for you and transfer the funds to your bank for a small cut of each transaction. An improvement over PayPal, these providers can offer better reporting. A downside to this method is that the registrant's statement will show a charge from "Your Vendor" instead of "Your Company," which can lead to confusion.
Your own Merchant Account	A merchant account is the most direct and sophisticated way to collect payments. This is just a bank account that can accept payments from the Internet. Having your own account not only puts your name on the registrant's credit card statement, but you will receive the funds in real time, improving your cash flow. When linked with event management software, you can automate refunds and get detailed reports that are already reconciled with your registration records. You'll have to apply for a merchant account and be approved, but Cvent, RegOnline and other online registration sites have several partners that can make the process quick and easy while providing you a very competitive rate.

Taking Care of the People and the Planet

Planning Responsibly

Social responsibility, being environmentally accountable, and taking into consideration cultural sensitives and ethics are just as important to event planning as dealing with the details. Simply put, by providing goods and services while using social, cultural, economic and environmentally sustainable business practices, one is thinking about the people, the planet and the future. To be responsible to the people and the planet, we must try to be sustainable and acknowledge and respect our differences. Event planners provide goods and services to people and places all around the planet and are situated to make a meaningful impact. Focusing on people as much as on the planet is important for our business. We must sustain our resources and make our planet a better place for all our citizens.

At any given moment there are thousands of meetings and events going on with millions of attendees traveling to and from different locales throughout the world. The events industry is perfectly situated to have an extraordinary environmental and social impact. Every change we cause will make a difference.

Our industry encompasses so many other industries and businesses that any change we make has a great deal of influence. We can exert considerable pressure on transportation, food and beverage industries, hotels, convention centers, the hospitality trade and other businesses we interact with. Every aspect of our business can play a role in sound environmental, cultural and social causes. This is a powerful position to be in, and we must take it seriously.

As event planners, you are in the perfect position to make a contribution to the health and sustainability of the planet and create a healthy living and economically sound environment. You also have an opportunity to educate everyone involved in the event industry along with each and every participant of your event. By changing the way you do business you can do a great deal to help your communities, people (including your employees), and the planet. You can make a difference to the people who need it the most right in the city you are holding your event.

The more you act responsibly, the more questions you ask and the more knowledgeable you become, the greater the impact you will have. We ultimately want to use our resources wisely and leave a lighter footprint on our communities, our cities and our planet. It is becoming popular to demonstrate social and environmental responsibility. It looks good for corporations and groups in general to be making socially responsible choices.

You may have to change your way of doing business as usual, but think of the rewards and the satisfaction you will reap knowing that you have contributed to saving resources instead of depleting or wasting valuable natural products. It takes a little more effort to plan a green event, arrange for a social act or do anything the unconventional way, but then again, you are event planners who are always up for the challenge, and being resourceful and creative is your hallmark.

Green Event Planning

Being socially responsible requires being environmentally sound in your decision-making process. This type of planning includes energy conservation, minimizing consumption of natural resources, reducing waste, recycling and using earth-friendly products. Designing an event by deliberately incorporating environmental plans in every stage of the process and minimizing any negative impact on the environment is being a conscientious planner. Whether you are choosing your destination or deciding on what food to serve, each choice is made with this consideration.

Events and meetings create huge amounts of waste. One event can leave behind tons of waste — food, cardboard, paper, Styrofoam and plastic. A few changes in one event alone can save trees, water or carbons and keep tons of waste from hitting our landfills. Try small steps at first, and see how easy it becomes after a while. You will feel so good about the results you will be eager to change another aspect of your business. Choose wisely.

Corporate Social Responsibility

Corporate Social Responsibility (CSR) is a concept whereby organizations voluntarily adopt interests of the communities in which they operate. It is a commitment to contribute to sustainable economic progress by working with employers, their families, the local community and society at large to improve lives.

Events are held in different locations other than where our offices are all the time. When we go to any place other than our own backyards, we are using their resources. Using CSR's is an opportunity to give back to these communities and the people who live there. But we need to give back to our own communities as well. By incorporating CSR's into our event planning process, we are able to make a difference that is beyond the single bottom line of profit.

Cultural Sensitivity, Diversity and Ethics

The world is shrinking and communities around the globe are growing more and more diverse. Because of this, we as event planners must become more culturally sensitive and create events that are inclusive of multiple philosophies, beliefs and values.

Ethics play an important role as event planners in our practice and for what we should expect from the participants who come to our events. We are often representatives of those who hire us, and we must conduct ourselves with honesty and integrity and provide a safe space for our attendees.

Planning for the Environment

Green meetings are very mainstream today, and they are continuing to evolve, so much so that venues, suppliers and participants are responding and cooperating. Because the public and planners are starting to be more ecologically educated, many suppliers — especially hotels and convention facilities — are upgrading their facilities, implementing more environmentally friendly processes and programs as well. The more you request and utilize these services, the more suppliers and vendors will incorporate green practices, too.

The first step is commitment. Whether you are an independent event planner or work for a company, you can develop and establish a baseline of criteria, policies, approaches and guiding principles as your standard practices. Depending on each situation, you can use all or some of these standards. The second is creating your standards (your green plan) and sharing them with everyone involved with the event, including your participants. Identify where you are willing to compromise since all standards will not be applicable at all times. Lastly, measure your results. You will be amazed at some of the facts and figures you find.

Is this event necessary?

This is the first question that should be considered. Do we need to do a face-to-face, or will another method of sharing the information suffice? We know that face-to-face meetings and gatherings of groups of people will never cease, but there are times when bringing your entire sales force together is not the best use of time and money. With today's awesome technology, meetings via phone and computer may be adequate.

Online meetings and conference calls are becoming more popular as technology improves and energy prices rise. It is common for corporations and businesses to have their regular business meetings via phone or computer. Webinars, webcasting, video streaming and teleconferences are a few of the more accepted and practical forms of meeting today, reducing travel, expenses, time and waste of natural resources.

Think locally

One decision you can make right up front is to buy local and use locally made products. For example, if your event is in California, do not have Maine lobster flown in. Use locally caught salmon or crabs from the nearest coastal city. Do not fly in a speaker from Florida when there are qualified speakers or entertainers in the city where you are hosting your event.

If you are in Santa Fe, do not use flowers grown in Hawaii. Decorate your event with local cacti and model your theme around them. Using non-local goods means you are wasting fossil fuels to fly in the products, creating extra packaging waste and additional expense for freight and travel. Better yet, by going local you are actually helping out the local community and its farmers, fishermen, artisans, craftspeople and businesspeople. You are helping to sustain their living. As for your guests, they benefit by experiencing the local flavor of the area and all the treasures it has to offer.

Even when your event is not local for you the planner, try to bring the flavor of the locale into the event by using the natural ambiance as your theme. You can actually save money by integrating the neighboring wares and goods into the food and décor to enhance your participants' experience and create a fond memory of the event.

Try specialty foods from the region or famous foods such as fresh crabs or oysters in San Francisco, halibut in Alaska, Texas beef barbecue in Houston, Boston Clam Chowder in New England, local lobster in Maine, or perhaps Cuban food in Florida. You get the picture.

Use the local flora and fauna for decorations and appeal. Do not have cut flower bouquets on the tables but potted flowers that can be given to the guests, local children's hospitals or retirement communities after the event. These are also perfect gifts or prizes for a raffle.

You can save on travel, hotel and food costs by using local speakers and entertainers. Instead of shipping everything to the out-of-town site, rent or buy locally. Think twice about having something specially made just for one event. Try to have signs made that can be reused for multiple occasions. Typically any manufactured item will generate 70 times its weight of waste during the manufacturing process.

The Green Game Plan

Setting environmental standards is a step toward becoming green. An important part of your responsibility as an event planner is making choices. Do you want chicken or beef? Shall we have a buffet or seated service? Will we have handouts or place the presentation on our website? What city is the best choice for this event? Shall we serve snacks at the breaks or just coffee? Paper or plastic? The decision-making process is endless. Every choice you make will have an environmental impact. When you set your own environmental standards, you can easily make consistent choices by putting them into practice. You will know where and on what you are willing to compromise.

How committed are you to greening your events? This level of commitment will direct your standards. What are your criteria for a green event? What are your priorities? Develop a plan outlining your standards, your commitments and your plans for implementing them. You will be able to use these guidelines when sending your request for proposal (RFP) to vendors, suppliers and venues.

Here are some of the most important areas that affect the people and the planet. How can you incorporate these into your event planning process? Look at each area below, and set your standards according to your capabilities. We can't always get what we want. But we can do the best we can.

Destination: Often the city has been chosen without your input, but if you have a say in the location, choosing a green destination will make your planning process much easier. If you are the one who selects the destination, choose a city that minimizes travel for participants and has everything you need locally. There are many ways you can transform any city to create a more socially conscious event. A few things to consider:

- Ask the local Convention and Visitors Bureau or Destination Management Company for a list or to find venues, properties, vendors and suppliers who meet your environmental standards.

- Look into the mass transit systems connecting the major venues with other transportation services.

- Is the city served by adequate airlines to allow for fewer flights and minimize layovers? If your destination requires extensive travel for participants, consider using "carbon offsetting" programs.

- Submit a Request for Proposal (RFP) with your environmental standards.

- Is the city walkable? Are there nearby attractions?

Accommodations: Hotels and resorts have come a long way to improve their conservation practices. There is a wide variation in environmental consciousness and business practices.

- Choose hotel and event venues that connect to the airport by mass transit and are within walking distance of one another.

- Ask venues for their in-house environmental policies and a description of the programs in place.

- Have hotels complete the checklist and detail their environmental performance. Give preference to those with the best scores.

- When doing a site visit, verify that your environmental standards will indeed be met.

- Choose a hotel that is willing to follow your standards if they have none of their own.

- Do they have a Corporate Social Responsibility (CSR)?

- Are they working with local charitable organizations?

Venue: Conference centers are also becoming more responsible. Here are tips to make sure your choice is a sound one and to encourage your venue to become more conscious.

- Choose a venue that is connected to the airport by mass transit and within walking distance of the hotel. Ask the hotel if they have van service.
- Request a copy of their environmental policy and plan.
- Find out what in-house environmental programs the venue offers.
- Perform a site visit to verify that your environmental service requirements can be met.
- Find out if the venue has had any environmental audits performed in the last five years. Ask to see the reports.
- Choose a venue that is willing to cooperate with your standards.
- Try to locate the hotel and meeting venue within walking distance of each other.
- Do they have an active CSR?

Transportation: One of the most significant environmental impacts of your meeting will result from how you move people around and how far they travel.

- Have those who cannot travel attend virtually by using new technology.
- Choose a destination with minimal travel requirements for participants.
- Communicate to the attendees the environmentally preferable transportation choices for getting to their destination. Commuter trains and other mass transit systems are preferable to car travel.
- If air travel is required, recommend an airline that has a sound environmental program.

- Make it easy for guests to get to the airport from the meeting venue. Provide information about the local public transit system, or arrange for carpooling shuttles.
- Purchase electronic tickets for airline tickets.
- If traveling by car, look for vehicles that reduce emissions: electric and hybrid-powered. Vehicles using natural gas, propane, methane gas and ethanol are good options.
- Provide a public transit pass and map in delegates' packages.
- Establish a carbon-neutral initiative to counteract the CO_2 emissions from your event.

Food and Beverage: By working closely with your food and beverage supplier, you can make some small changes that have a big impact.

- Ask that condiments, beverages and other food items be provided in bulk instead of individually packaged.
- Do not serve water in individual plastic bottles.
- Ensure food and beverage packaging is recyclable and that it will be recycled.
- Give your delegates reusable coffee mugs at the start of the conference.
- Ask your supplier to buy local produce in season to avoid costly transportation of goods.
- Offer fair trade, shade-grown and organic coffee.
- Request organic produce and free-range chicken/eggs/meats.
- Offer vegetarian meal selections. Vegetables consume less land and energy to produce.
- Request participants to sign up for meals. Letting you know how many meals they will be requiring will reduce food waste and your costs.
- Have untouched food donated to a local food bank or soup kitchen.

- Ask that leftover food be composted or shipped to a local farm as livestock feed.
- Use reusable cutlery, dishware and linens.
- Choose reusable centerpieces and decorations such as living plants or silk flowers. Give these away as table prizes.

Communications and Marketing: Your communications and marketing are a chance for you to make your environmental and social efforts known, and using new media and electronic delivery can also save you some money.

- Share your standards with all those involved: management, suppliers, participants, presenters, entertainment and exhibitors.
- Use social networking, the web and email to promote your event.
- Use electronic registration, and publish the agenda online.
- When hard copy material is necessary, print on both sides, and use soy- or vegetable-based inks and recycled, chlorine-free paper.
- Ask your venue to dedicate a TV channel to announce information and updates.
- Avoid paper duplication by giving participants their packages when they check in rather than before.
- Offer electronic proceedings of the events.
- Ask presenters to minimize paper hand-outs.
- Present speakers' notes electronically along with conference minutes.
- Use your leverage with your contracted services, and encourage them to go green with their communications.

Exhibition Production: Including your exhibitors and facilities in your standards eliminates unnecessary waste.

- Ask them to create signs for reuse.
- Provide collection bins for recycling name tags and any other paper goods they won't be taking home.

Tell your exhibitors about your standards. Get them involved by asking them to:

- Print their materials on recycled paper, and use vegetable-based inks.
- Bring only what is needed to the event, and take away what they do not give out.
- Use items for the free handouts and trinkets that are made from recycled materials, durable or reusable.
- Promote their environmental initiatives.
- Use technology for promotion when possible to eliminate paper waste.

Bring the facility on board. Request that:

- They provided on-site recycling for paper, cans, glass and other materials that are generated.
- They choose reusable decorations and display materials.
- Ask local schools, retirement facilities or charitable organizations if they would like to receive used decorations after the event.
- Provide separate receptacles for recyclables and the garbage.
- Request that the display booths be created using recycled, reusable material.

Beyond Recycling

Research shows that during a typical five-day conference, 2,500 attendees may use 62,500 plates, 87,500 napkins, 75,000 glasses or cups, and 90,000 bottles or cans. Is this something we have a say about? Absolutely!

Multiply those items by thousands of attendees and exhibitors, and you can have several tons of waste produced from just one major event. The good news is that as meeting planners, you can find ways to reduce the waste produced at all of your events, large and small.

You can do something simple such as requesting that your participants recycle. Put the request in brochures and agendas. Make announcements to remind people to recycle. Have visible bins for cans, bottles and paper. Collect and reuse tote bags and name badges. These are very easy remedies to filling the landfills with unnecessary waste.

The next step in green thinking following recycling is to use alternatives. The emphasis is now on conserving our resources, efficiency in usage, reducing consumption, re-usage of products and recycling. Instead of plastic or paper plates that can be recycled, use glass or china dishes. Free yourself from having to recycle at all.

By using the following straightforward tactics, one event with 23,000 participants and 100 exhibitors were able to recycle more than 26 tons of waste and achieve a waste diversion rate of 95 percent. It saved about 238 trees, 4,300 gallons of water and nearly 30 cubic yards of landfill space. Now that is progress! The event planners worked in partnership with the venue to promote recycling, and they made the following few effortless changes to achieve the above outstanding results.

- Replaced the non-recyclable Styrofoam cups and plates with plastic or glass ones.

- Trained all staff appropriately and got them invested in the program and excited about the intentions.

- Installed customized three-bin separated waste containers for bottles and cans, paper, and organic waste at all concessions and food service locations.

- Supervised the docks to ensure departing exhibitors used the correct bin and knew what materials to take back home with them.

- Enlightened the participants and exhibitors ahead of time that recycling was an important aspect of the event. They placed recycling information in the registration materials, brochures and agendas.

All of these strategies and more can be integrated into any event regardless of size, location, number of people, or purpose. You can create this environmental atmosphere no matter what your event is all about.

Location: Wing of a large convention center
Number of participants: 800 attendees
Type of Event: All day seminars and workshops with lunch

When greening events was in its infancy stages, a very reputable meeting planning organization was holding one of their annual all-day seminars. They did everything right. They picked a newly built LEED Certified convention center, chose local food choices for the lunch menu, eliminated water bottles completely and replaced them with water stations, handed out bags made of recycled material, served lunch buffet style on compostable dining ware and encouraged ride sharing to the event.

The problem (as small as it was) with compostable dining ware is that it is important to keep it separated from the regular trash. There were a few signs on tables, but it was very evident that people did not know what to do once they arrived at the trash containers. Wanting to do it "right," the participants stood at the bins (which were poorly marked) and couldn't figure out where to throw them. It was a funny sight and a perfect candid camera moment. But probably not for the eco-minded attendee who just wanted to do it correctly.

The moral of this story is to have sufficient signage, let the attendees know even before they come and/or have someone next to the bins direct people toward what to do. It was good for event planners because they were able to be a part of the change and hopefully take the information with them to their next event.

Connie Mack
Sacramento, CA

Carbon Offsets

There will always be travel of some kind in the meeting and event business, and thousands of participants, staff, speakers and entertainers will travel by airplane, car, bus and even train. As we have said, the first step is to choose a convenient destination where fewer people travel long distances to get there.

To compensate for whatever travel does take place, buying carbon to replace emissions is a way to counter-balance negative impact from the travel. Carbon offsetting erases the impact of your trip by reducing carbon emissions somewhere in the world in proportion to the damage caused by your travels. For instance, it would cost about $5.50 to offset the carbon used for a round trip from San Francisco to Orlando, Florida for one person.

Organizations that can help reduce your carbon footprint and support climate-friendly projects are easy to find. Depending on where you make a donation, the money is used for conserving forests for their climate benefits, building wind farms in India or the United States, restoring the rainforest in Uganda, installing energy efficient lighting in South Africa, providing energy-efficient stoves in Madagascar, or funding a renewable farm methane project in the Midwest. There are hundreds of projects going on around the world. It is your choice of who to support. When you buy a carbon offset, your money is used to fund projects that reduce emissions on your behalf. Do a search to find the organization that fits your event or your company style.

Today, the discussion most often focuses on aviation emissions. But aviation is responsible for less than 5 percent of worldwide emissions. However, with the expected increase in air traffic over the next 20 years, CO_2 emissions caused by aviation could double without intervention.

How does carbon offsetting help fight climate change?

Carbon offsets are an easy and cost effective way for any person or business to take action to stop global warming caused by the buildup of greenhouse gases in the atmosphere from human activity. It enables individuals and businesses to reduce their CO2 emissions by displacing the CO2 elsewhere, typically where it is more economical to do so.

Carbon offsets include renewable energy, energy efficiency, forest protection and reforestation projects. As more and more people are concerned about global warming and seek to reduce their climate impact, carbon offsets, along with personal carbon reductions, offer an important counteractive balance to global warming.

Carbon offset providers often provide a "carbon calculator" for individuals to estimate the carbon dioxide emissions arising from their consumption of electricity, gas and air travel. You can suggest that participants look into making a donation, you can split the costs, or you can have a sponsor pick up the tab for the entire number of guests. You will be doing your part in reducing emissions.

Using carbon offsetting within your business can have benefits for you. It is a great public relations approach. You can demonstrate your responsiveness and willingness to make a global difference to your target market, clients, attendees and colleagues. Put in writing that you are donating to a fund or that your sponsor is donating. Use the information in the marketing material, the material provided at the event, on your website, and on signs at the event. If you do not want to pick up the entire tab, you can provide donation envelopes to your participants who can play a part if they want. If nothing else, it spreads the news. The changes would be dramatic if everyone contributed just a little to making a difference.

Look for organizations that offer assistance such as the Cleaner and Greener, aProgram of Leonardo Academy, Inc. Cleaner and Greener calculates emissions caused by:

- Electricity and fuel use during the event
- Travel to and from the event
- Food preparation and cleanup for event meals
- Electricity used in hotel rooms

Reducing all types of emissions is important. The pollution caused by energy use includes carbon dioxide, particulate matter, nitrogen oxides and sulfur dioxide. Each type of pollution causes its own particular set of environmental and health problems, so offsetting all different types of pollution caused by energy use is important for environmental improvement. The results have lasting effects on people around the globe.

Organizations that register their event with Cleaner and Greener Event Certification make a commitment to work with the program to gather emission use and to offset the emissions caused by energy use associated with their event. If you want to sign up to have your event certified, the group will help you to lessen the environmental impact of your event, provide you with copy for your marketing material and participants handouts, provide pre-and post-event emission statistics, and even assist in processing tax-deductible donations. This is just one example of the types of organizations doing this type of work.

Event: Jim and Nancy's Environmental Wedding
Venue: Outdoor Public Park
Participants: 150 guests

When we decided to marry, we carried our strong environmental beliefs into the planning of our wedding. Here are some of the changes we incorporated that gave our wedding a social theme.

Our announcements were eco-friendly invitations from a green company, and they used the company's line of Grow-a-Note products. They were made from recycled paper printed with soy-based inks and embedded with a mixture of wildflower seeds. After the wedding, guests could plant the invitations in soil and watch flowers bloom. They were beautiful invitations.

At the celebration, we spent four hours eating and drinking. Four hours! We had the caterer use only locally grown vegetables and fresh caught fish, and, oh yes, a chocolate fountain for the children. We didn't want to be short on food and fun, but we just were conscious about what we chose to eat, drink and how we decorated. Any leftover food went to the local homeless shelter, and the flowers were taken to the children's wing of our local hospital. We picked the flowers from our garden and asked the floral designer to enhance the arrangements with other local flowers.

For those who traveled from out of town, we asked them to contribute to an environmentally friendly organization instead of getting a gift for us. After the honeymoon, we calculated the travel for our guests and our honeymoon and then wrote a check to *The Pacific Forest Trust* to balance out our impact.

It could have been easy enough to eliminate the environmental impact by eliminating the party, but that would prevent us from sharing our happiness with the people we love best. And that is certainly not the point. It is to celebrate joyfully but consciously.

Nancy K. C.
Sebastopol, CA

Green Venues and Locations

Cities, hotels, conference centers, cruise ships, clubs and even restaurants are becoming more environmental as a normal way of business. They have found it to be a cost-cutting venture and a great public relations tool. It also creates goodwill among citizens, employees, clients, sponsors, etc., saves resources, and is just the responsible thing to do. Studies show that socially and environmentally responsible companies are inclined to prefer a green venue over a traditional one.

When the property has a good reputation for green practices, it will attract like-minded organizations, environmental groups, conservation organizations, governmental entities, and educational groups to use that venue. As this trend gathers awareness and momentum, more and more groups will require environmental practices from their venues.

Beware of Green Washing. Watch what a venue says about their environmental practices. It is easy to use the word "green" because it covers everything from global warming to recycled paper. Look a little deeper into the practices of each venue.

There are dozens and dozens of American and International convention and conference centers that currently identify themselves as environmental. Look for LEED (Leadership in Energy and Environmental Design) properties. Some are much more advanced in the environmental arena than others. Throughout the United States and around the world, cities are finding it important that when upgrading or building new convention centers, hotels, restaurants and sports facilities, environmental concerns are on the top of their list. It not only saves money in the long run but it promotes good public relations.

Do your homework, and ask questions. Most venues are proud of their accomplishments in this area, and you can find what they have done to environmentally upgrade their property on their websites. If not obvious, be sure to ask the sales team at your prospective venues.

As for cities around the United States, there are several very environmentally and socially conscious cities. You should check with Convention and Visitor Bureaus (CVBs) to find out about the next city where you book your event. The top rated "green" city in 2009 was Portland, Oregon. In 2015, it is New York City with San Francisco, then and now, running second. They are on the list for many reasons, but how they affect us as event planners has to do with transportation to the venue from the airport, availability of local and fresh food, number of venues who are participating in the environmental movement, and much more.

Other cities that make the list are Boston; Seattle; Philadelphia; Denver; Chicago; Austin, Texas; Minneapolis; Baltimore; Branson, Missouri; Vancouver, British Columbia; Cambridge, Massachusetts; Oakland, California; Raleigh, North Carolina; Honolulu; and Eugene, Oregon. Do your research; changes are being made daily! If you can't choose the city you are traveling to, then be sure to research the venue.

Hotels and hotel chains have also joined in the green movement. I want to mention Hyatt since they were one of the first major chains to have, in writing, environmental standards for each of their hotels. Others have definitely come on board throughout the years and have aggressive plans in place for both the citizens and the environment. Again, do your research and ask the venue directly to see their green plan and CSRs. If you don't have say in the city or the venue and find that the venue doesn't practice anything mentioned here, go ahead and ask for some changes while your group is there.

As an example, Economically Sound Company has an eco-program called Green Suites International. In one year alone, their hotel clients collectively replaced some 250,000-plus lights with energy-efficient bulbs, saving more than 70 trillion kilowatt hours of electricity and avoiding 7 million tons of carbon dioxide emissions every year from coal-fired power plants. They have implemented water-efficient guest room solutions such as sink aerators and low-flow shower heads, saving an estimated 250 million gallons of water per year. By installing more than 10,000 Guestat Energy Management Systems, they saved 10 trillion kilowatt hours of electricity and avoided 5 billion tons of carbon dioxide emissions every year.

They added more than 14,000 bathroom amenity dispensers, annually diverting more than 10 million plastic bottles from landfills. In adopting a linen-and-towel reuse program, they conserved more than 100 million gallons of water a year. What is your venue doing?

Ask your participants to participate in green travel!

Now that you have done all that you can to be more conscious in your planning process it is time to ask your participants to join in the movement. This is a request or a suggestion that can go out to your attendees prior to their departure for your event, again at the event, and something that you can share with them after the event.

This is a long list and not all suggestions are appropriate for your particular situation. Obviously, some of these suggestions are for participants coming to stay for at least one night. Use those that will work for your travelers.

When preparing and packing for your trip:

- Pack your own personal amenities.
- Purchase and re-use 3 oz. containers and refill at home with shampoo, conditioner and lotion (Especially if you carry on your luggage).
- For airline or rental car confirmations, print only the first page or two at the most.
- Reserve a car with good fuel economy.

Upon arrival at the front desk:

- Take just the key, and leave the packet. If you are traveling alone, ask for one key, and turn it in at the desk when you check out.
- Ask them to keep their guest room map along with any unnecessary extra paperwork they are handing out.
- If possible, take the stairs or escalator to get to your room.

In your guest room:

- Decline housekeeping service and turn-down service if your stay is short.
- Only use the towels and washcloths that you need. Leave all other towels untouched (and set aside) so that Housekeeping will know they were not used.
- When you are done with a towel, hang it up to dry for re-use during short stays.
- If you are alone in a room with two double beds, don't mess up the bedspread and sheets on the second bed.
- For men, fill the sink bowl when shaving versus running the water.
- For women, turn the shower off when shaving and rinse off later.
- Turn the water off when brushing teeth!

During your stay:

- Turn the lights and television off when leaving your room, especially when you check out.
- Turn the air conditioner up or down, according to the season, when leaving the room.
- During summer months, close the drapes to keep the sun's heat out. During winter months, open your drapes to help heat the room during the day.
- Tell hotel managers to adjust the air conditioning in the public areas, such as the lobby and banquet rooms, according to comfort levels.
- When ordering room service, tell them not to send any extra food items or condiments you don't need.
- If you drink your coffee black, tell them to hold the cream. If you don't want your side orders of toast, rolls, etc., tell them not to send it.
- Ask your room service waiter if the condiments that are sent are going to be reused. If so, send them back, or take them home.

At any restaurant or bar:

- Order off the buffet, or order the specials of the day, as these represent foods purchased and prepared in bulk.
- Drink draft beer and carbonated soda from the fountain rather than the bottle, as this saves a lot of energy and fuel in avoiding manufacturing and transporting all that extra packaging.
- When you do have to buy bottled water, buy the local brand.
- Don't take extra napkins. If they are given to you anyway, save them for reuse later.
- Decline stir sticks when ordering a drink at the bar or even a coffee. Likewise, don't take a lid or straw for your beverage unless you need to.

Miscellaneous:

- If you happen upon a hotel making Green effort, reward them with comment cards and feedback. If you are at a hotel that shows no effort, take a moment to fill out the comment card and let them know this cause is important enough for you to change your future travel buying habits.
- Where possible, consume foods that are produced locally.
- If your hotel is one of the few that have already implemented a guest recycling program, be sure to use it and thank management for their efforts. If recycling is not available, mention it to the hotel management in person or on your comment card.
- Avoid the use of Styrofoam cups and containers whenever possible. Carry and use a reusable coffee mug. If you have to use Styrofoam, ask the server to refill your cup versus wasting another.

These may seem petty, but every little bit helps, and people like being asked to participate.

Social Responsibility

Everything that has been written in this section so far is a form of corporate social responsibility. Being environmentally conscious in everything you plan puts you ahead of the game. Corporate social responsibility (CSR), also known as corporate conscience, corporate citizenship, or corporate social performance, is a voluntary business practice in which the focus is not only on profits but also on the effect those profits are having on the rest of the world. Companies with this approach embrace responsibility for the impact their company has on the environment, consumers, employees and communities around them and actively take steps to improve them by giving back in some way. It is the triple bottom line: People, Planet and Profit.

It is not just corporate. Social responsibility can be integrated into local, personal and community events as well. CSR policies demonstrate credibility and trustworthiness to clients and can set you apart in the market.

What does it really mean to be socially responsible? The John F. Kennedy School of Government at Harvard University says corporate social responsibility encompasses not only what companies do with their profits but also how they make them. It goes beyond philanthropy and compliance and addresses how companies manage their economic, social and environmental impacts, in addition to their relationships in all key spheres of influence: the workplace, the marketplace, the supply chain, the community and the public policy realm. As event planners, it is our responsibility to fit this into our overall mission and purpose.

In practical terms, this means that companies and event leaders commit themselves to being good citizens by following environmental and other sustainability principles such as:

- Consume as few resources as possible
- Encourage employees and participants to contribute to their community
- Work only with suppliers and partners that fit specific social, ethical and environmental criteria
- Advocate for broader social development

How does this work at an event? Starting small is a good idea. Continuing to build and improve upon the program is your goal. Sometimes it isn't obvious, but through creative brainstorming, you can create phenomenal opportunities for connection. First things first.

- Establish a cause that fits into your company's purpose and find existing products or services to fit that of a charitable organization or community in need.
- Be relevant to the markets your company operates in.
- Provide the opportunity to engage employees, customers and other event attendees in participation.

Make sure all attendees can contribute in a tangible way. They can contribute in one or several ways including:

- Donating money
- Volunteering time
- Donating goods and services
- Helping with the organization of the fund raiser

For example, if your company manufactures paint, paint brushes and paint products, a fitting service project would be to paint a school or home for a low-income family or the elderly. Or maybe it means the attendees at a meeting create art projects to be donated to a hospital in the area, or that you put on how-to clinics on transforming a wall of graffiti into a community mural.

Another example could be an afternoon working on a Habitat for Humanity worksite or going to a local food bank and packaging boxes of food for the needy. Or perhaps arranging a reading fair for kids in disadvantaged neighborhoods where your attendees can donate books and be readers. Think of the help needed after both Katrina and the BP oil spill. The beach communities could have used assistance. The possibilities are endless.

You can create a very interactive event that will make a lasting impact on a community in need, transform your participants, and position your company as a socially responsible organization. These ideas can be used for small events as well. The important thing to think about is how you and your event can make life better for others.

Here is an example of the best a city can offer a meeting planner. This is on the Web page of Kissimmee, Florida. It makes the event planner's job very easy.

Under the Heading of "Corporate & Social Responsibility"

Kissimmee believes strongly in the value of both people and natural resources. Accordingly, the Kissimmee CVB proudly embraces the Corporate Social Responsibility (CSR) concept, and we encourage those who meet in Kissimmee to include community service as a part of a complete meeting's agenda. The Kissimmee CVB can help identify worthy local charities and community projects, offering your delegates the opportunity for volunteerism or donation. Several groups are listed here, and the Kissimmee CVB can assist with the right selection for your needs.

It is said that volunteerism promotes goodwill and is personally fulfilling. It will heighten a person's awareness of community needs and inspire further action — additional volunteering, donating financial resources, advocating for a cause, and even making sure everyday actions benefit the greater good. The benefits are endless.

Volunteerism is also known to be addictive and contagious with the majority of volunteers repeating their service and bringing friends and family along to help. When attendees see what an impact a couple of hours can do for a community, they start to understand what CSR is about.

Event: Two-day seminar
Location: Resort Hotel
Participants: Meeting Planners
Numbers: 30
Lesson: Practice what you preach

I was asked to speak to a small group of specifically chosen meeting planners regarding planning with the people and planet in mind. We all would be traveling out of our state to meet at a resort.

I wanted to put my actions where my words were. Just speaking about and telling stories about *Event Planning with Responsibility* didn't look as effective or make as great of an impact as actually doing something.

I looked online at all the non-profit organizations in the city I would be speaking in. Since 99 percent of my participants were women, I decided on a shelter for abused women. They helped women get back into the workplace after some time of rehabilitation. One of their main sources of funding came from clothing donations sales.

I looked into how they did their business and really liked what they did. I called the director and said I'd be in town with a group women, how could we help? And would you like to come address the group and let them know what you do and how their contribution would help? I also asked for information that I could email out prior to their arrival.

When I told the director what hotel we were meeting at, she was even more excited to tell me that her non-profit and our hotel had an ongoing relationship of fund raising. She had a good relationship with the general manager and director of sales. They had already formed a great partnership.

I emailed the participants with the information regarding the non-profit and asked them to bring clothes, jewelry, shoes, handbags, or if they preferred, they could give money when they arrived.

The participants were informed with enough time to prepare. They brought appropriate donations.

The director arrived on the afternoon of the last day, gave an introductory speech, and the participants in turn gave her either goods or money. The rewards were smiles and feelings of accomplishment throughout the room for everyone. Attendees know that they made a difference in the lives of others, and it makes them feel good. Hopefully, they will take those good feelings home with them and do community service in their own communities.

Shannon

Many studies have shown that when you witness or hear about an act of compassion, one is more likely to emulate it.

Creating Partnerships

Building partnerships with those you do business with is the key to creating the most environmentally friendly and socially conscious events possible — each and every time. Working with others is a daily undertaking in our industry. We interact with and do business with our co-workers and management, numerous vendors and suppliers, sponsors, our clientele, and often with other organizations and meeting planners when we produce our events. Each individual or company we deal with has an integral role to the success of our event, which means each should be on board when it comes to being environmental and sustainable. By collectively striving for the same results and goals, we generate binding and lasting partnerships with those we work with.

How do we go about generating these partnerships with those we work with regardless of who they are and the roles they play? If it is our desire to become more environmentally and socially conscious, then it is our responsibility to educate others about our goals and new practices. So first we must develop our own foundation and describe what that means in writing and then share with the others we cooperate with.

Building a green team with an environmental purpose and a socially responsible team from within your company with your own associates is the first and foremost partnership to form. While we depend upon and rely on other people, companies and organizations that we have worked with for years, we must have a solid set of guidelines and standards from within our own companies and organizations in order to ask others to join us in our new direction. The policies and procedures must come from you first — from the partnerships you have created with your co-workers and colleagues.

Delegate responsibility to yourself or a co-worker to form teams and begin to establish the guidelines and standards and policy and procedures. Get the buy-in from your colleagues and management and then share with the others involved in the decision-making process and the direct reports. Your initiatives should feel like a natural extension of your current policies and procedures. Keep it simple, but make it relevant. It's critically important to engage your entire organization in your initiatives and bring them in on the purpose you have established.

When it comes to creating partnerships with outside vendors, suppliers and other planners, communication is the key. It is imperative that you communicate with your current vendors and suppliers your new purpose and ask them if they have initiatives of their own or if they are willing to adopt some of yours. Many may be reluctant to do so because of lack of education and experience.

One of the biggest challenges is this resistance because they believe it is going to cost them more money. To overcome these challenges, you must begin the conversation and be equipped with answers to the litany of questions that are bound to come up. This new way of being and doing will require education on everyone's part. This is a good partnership when you work together as a team.

You can either educate them, ask them to make some changes, or find other vendors who will. But the last thing you want to do is lose a good resource because we know how hard breaking in a new vendor and establishing a new relationship can be. So the best solution is to bring people on board and train them if necessary. Some of your vendors may already have their own policies and procedures and without having a conversation, you won't know about them. So ask, and maybe together you can come up with solutions and answers. This is how the partnerships between all of your business relationships are established. The winning strategy is to make sure everyone involved with your event is on the same page.

Make your partnerships real, and make sure your associates are dependable and responsible enough to follow through. Sometimes this means getting these agreements and policies into the contracts. Do not be afraid to put your requirements in writing. Negotiate until you are satisfied with the results. We know that circumstances will arise where our initiatives will not fit into a particular event, but we can come close or compromise. Good negotiation skills and good contracts are imperative at this juncture.

Culture, Diversity and Ethics

The issue of culture, diversity and inclusion rises and falls for our industry as it does worldwide. With changing patterns of immigration, all countries need to consider the impact of cultural diversity on their businesses. As planners, we need to consider how to reflect the diversity of those who attend our events, buy products and book venues. We should also look to the future when thinking about those we want to attract and be inclusive in marketing images.

Ethics also plays a big role in how we present ourselves, the companies we work for, the vendors we use, and the participants who come to our events. We need to be upfront, honest and treat everyone with respect. Integrity should be one of our main goals in every decision we make.

Cultural Sensitivity and Diversity

Our communities, towns and cities, and the world at large are becoming more and more diverse. Now, more than ever, the hospitality industry must change and adapt along with these transforming times. This means we need to be aware in all aspects of our planning process. Diversity should play a factor in our event planning team, the choices of locations and venues, our speakers and entertainment selections, and our food and beverage choices.

For example, if your event falls on a religious holiday because no other date was plausible, how can you accommodate those attendees who follow that religion? Some thought should always go into picking dates, but it is impossible to always find the perfect date that suits everyone. If you have to use dates that coincide with a holiday, make sure to let your participants know that you are aware and will try to accommodate them.

This goes for Sabbath and Sunday services as well. You may not be able to rearrange your agenda, but you might want to acknowledge and apologize.

Think about the food and beverage choices when ordering. People have such diverse eating habits, food sensitivities, dietary restrictions, and cultural rituals these days that your selection of meals, breaks foods and vendor choices is extremely important. As much as you can, find out what is on or off the accepted list of foods for your participants. Meals are an important part of many events and can either be remembered in a favorable or negative light. The more you know about your participants needs, the more favorable the memory will be.

When looking for properties or venues, locations that have trained staff in cultural understanding and sensitivity should be high on your list. Training that promotes understanding of varied cultures is a key component to happy and comfortable guests.

Also think about culture and diversity in your marketing efforts. If using photos of people, make sure those images represent all of your diverse audience. Not only are the obvious color differences important but choose photos with younger or older people and different body types and abilities. Try to be as inclusive as possible with a wide variety of images.

If you want to attract this wide array of participants, be sure your event can accommodate them. If you promote a person in a wheelchair through your images, be sure your venue is compliant with the Americans with Disabilities Act (ADA). If you want foreign-speaking attendees, will you have an interpreter? Think along these lines.

Other things to consider when choosing a particular state or country outside of the United States are their laws and how the event might look to your participants. Some states and countries have laws that may go against everything your group of attendees stand for. For example, even though gay marriage is legal in all 50 states, many still discriminate against LGBT citizens by denying workplace equality, the ability to adopt, or even housing. You can see how that might affect certain groups.

Women are treated as second-class citizens in many places around the world and even in many of our states. You may want to avoid holding an event someplace where that is happening if your participants are mostly women. Religious freedom is being suppressed in many places as well, so it would be prudent to take into consideration these big-picture ideals and sensitivities when choosing your location. I don't mean to talk politics here, but that is also an issue that is important to consider. Would it be wrong to have a Planned Parenthood conference at a Trump hotel? You decide.

Remember that you are bringing money into these states and countries where you hold your event. Be sure that your attendees are not offended by any laws and choose not to attend because they don't want their dollars going to states where they do not feel welcome.

Ethics

Planners often make decisions with large financial implications. Vendors try to get your business in many ways. It can be through kickbacks, tickets to the opera, or box seats at the football game. Where do you draw the line when accepting gifts offered by vendors, clients and suppliers? When confronted with the choice of taking an incentive, bribe or gift from a supplier, consider the consequences of your actions.

Can it affect your reputation if everyone knew about it? Is it reasonable and fair, or is it extravagant? Is it in violation of someone's trust? What is the intention and spirit in which it is given? Is it inappropriate, unfair, and only for personal gain? How do you feel about it? If you have any negative feeling about it, do not do it. It is not right for you.

Familiarization trips are typically multi-day, all-expenses-paid trips to inspect properties and destination cities. This is a very common offer to planners to get familiar with what a site or city has to offer. The question you need to ask yourself is: Are you seriously considering this city and venue? Is this destination right for your client? If not, then your intentions may be unethical. Doing a dry run for an event is an industry norm.

Kickbacks or rebates are also common in several businesses in the hospitality industry. Hotels may give rebates on sleeping room counts, transportation companies may offer a 10 percent kickback on total sales, or a travel agent may give free tickets as incentive. These are common, but how far should you go with them?

It is not black and white. The lines can be blurred. It depends on how you feel at the end of the day. Did everyone get the best deal? Did you compromise yourself in any way? Is it a win-win for all? Is this something you have to hide, or can you share it with others without guilt? These questions and more should be considered before you say yes to an offer that may be unethical.

A good rule of thumb is to let your client know that you were offered these trade norm incentives. Just be honest and you will have no qualms about accepting these offerings. As an industry, we want to be perceived as professional and be able to charge and receive fair compensation for our expertise and knowledge. We must hold ourselves to high ethical standards and practices. Avoid putting yourself, your company or client, or your suppliers at personal or professional risk by partaking in unethical behavior.

Early in my career, I was responsible for the logistics of a very large multi-day conference. One of my responsibilities was to find bus transportation for 800 people from eight different hotels traveling round-trip each day. As I was obtaining bids, one bus company offered me, as the coordinator, a 10 percent bonus fee. Wow. That was a substantial amount of money, especially since I was on a small hourly wage. After wrestling with my intention, I took the situation to my clients and asked what they thought. It would have been so easy to take the money, but my conscience bothered me. They ultimately said to pick the best company for the job and take a bonus if I was offered it. Indeed, I found the best company for the job and received a bonus. I slept well at night. It was a win-win situation.

Cindy M.
Jacksonville, Florida

Another area that you should be careful with and aware of because of its potential ethical consequences is intellectual property. Sometimes the line is a very fine one, so be clear about boundaries when using others' ideas, quotes, music, graphics, photos, etc.

If your group is social media savvy, it is good to set guidelines. Ask your group to be respectful, kind and honest. Express the importance of NOT defaming, blatantly lying or unfairly criticizing when sharing their experience. Even though you do not have control of this, you can ask or set protocols when your participants share their experience with the world.

High Level Logistics

Get Down to Business

At this point in the planning process, you should have your defined purpose, goals and objectives, financial goals, environmental standards and defined CSRs, meaningful discussions on culture and diversity, and preliminary work done on your budget. You have the "why." Now it is time to get the "when, where and how." With some of the major decisions completed, it is time to get down to some specifics. At this point, you need to pick time and date, decide on your destination (city, state or country) and location (venue or outdoor space), start to choose your speakers and entertainers, and create your agenda.

Do not take this section lightly. It will determine the success or failure of your event. Will you meet your goals and objectives? Will your participants walk away from this event satisfied that they got what they came for, and will they receive what you promised them? Will you make that return on investment that you planned for?

Everything you decide to do pertaining to this section will be used and reflected in the creation of your marketing and promotional materials and your social media and networking. You will use this information to design your agendas. It will affect your budget, influence who your participants are, and touch every other detail regarding your event.

Date and Time Selection

Picking specific dates and times for your event is crucial to attracting participants to your event. Whether it is four days long or two hours, the event will start on a specific day at a specific time and end on a specific day at a specific time. You will want to do some research prior to deciding on these specifics since they are central to your success. Be sure that similar events are not happening around the same time, and double check that the dates will not interfere with your participants' other commitments. Take into consideration holidays or special seasons.

Can you imagine how many tax accountants would come to your event on April 10th? Avoid a conflict in dates with your intended audience whenever possible. It might be ineffective to hold a 10-mile run in San Francisco the same weekend as the famous 105-year-old Bay to Breakers or to plan a medical conference the same month as the annual American Medical Association Convention. You do not need the competition for participants. Try to choose dates when your attendees have an open calendar.

Often the date is already established and non-negotiable. If so, you have to work around that date—not vice versa. Annual events often are the same day in the same week of the same month every year. A fixed date has advantages and disadvantages. If you wanted a specific venue but it was previously reserved for that time, you are out of luck. You cannot change the date to fit the venue.

Check all available sources for other events scheduled in the area. Talk with the convention bureaus in the area where you are holding your event. Peruse the Internet for dozens of topics related to your event, and look for similar events going on either locally or nationally. Take into consideration major holidays, religious observations, school breaks and extra-long weekends. Do not overlap with something that is already on the calendar of your potential participants.

Other thoughts to take into consideration when choosing the time and date for your events are: What days would be best? Would midweek be better than a Thursday, Friday or weekend? Where are your participants coming from? If people are traveling, take into consideration travel time, costs, and work schedules.

Early morning may be better to start your meeting if late afternoon traffic is a nightmare in your area. Fridays may be a hard day to keep your participants at the event and paying attention. By noon they may be planning an early escape to start the weekend. For special events, midweek or Saturdays and nights draw the most people. Again, ask a few questions. Will they be coming from work? Will they need to change their clothes before the event? What time do they get off work? Will traffic be an issue for the participants and volunteers? Will their partners be invited? Will they come in separate cars? Will there be enough parking? Consider all the possible problems or issues that can hinder your participants' attendance, and choose your dates and times accordingly.

When picking a date for an athletic event called "Run from Your Taxes," we picked April 15, which fell on a Saturday. I thought, how perfect, everyone would be done with their taxes and want to get outside for a fun run. I thought the registration form was clever. It was nearly identical to the 1040 tax form. The idea was brilliant. The form looked great. I did the same promotion and marketing that I had done for several other fun runs and was expecting about 200 people to register.

To my surprise, enrollment was so low that I ended up canceling the event. What I thought was a great idea others obviously did not. Perhaps I should have asked others for their take on the date and idea. Many people finish their taxes at the last minute and might not be in the mood for fun. The course was a public area, the permit was inexpensive, and the marketing material was reasonable. Fortunately, I was only out a small amount of money.

Lessons Learned: Pick your dates with care

Vicki M., Special Events
Portland, Oregon

MONEY SAVING TIPS

➠ Check the city's travel tax rate. At the time of this writing, the most expensive cities include Portland, Oregon; Chicago; Boston; Indianapolis; Columbus, Ohio; Minneapolis; and Washington, D.C. The lowest overall taxes are in Fort Lauderdale, Tampa and Fort Meyers, Florida; Detroit; San Diego; Ontario; Los Angeles; Orange County; Burbank, California; and Honolulu.

➠ Pick dates in the slow season. Generally, January and February are slower months excluding Florida, Hawaii and Southern California. Booking the event when the facility needs business is a great opener for negotiating deals.

➠ Booking around holidays such as Easter, Memorial Day and Labor Day might be to your advantage.

➠ Pick days of the week that are slower, such as Sundays. A multi-day conference arriving on Sunday and departing on Wednesday could earn you substantial savings.

➠ For one-day meetings, Monday and Friday are slower, and you can possibly get lower rates.

➠ If you can be flexible with dates and days of the week, ask the hotel for dates with the best rates.

➠ Do not be afraid to ask for better rates, especially if you are planning the event next week or next month. Facilities want to fill their rooms.

➠ Use the same facility for numerous events. They are likely to give you a better rate if you are a regular client.

➠ Consider dates when the venue has a high vacancy rate. You may be able to negotiate better rates and other benefits.

➠ Airfare is lower with a Saturday night stay.

➠ Negotiate some freebies such as complimentary suites, free parking, health club passes or airport transportation.

➠ Room rental fee can be waived if your block of room nights are picked up. Ask the hotel what that number is.

➠ Complimentary rooms — The usual ratio is 1:40 but ask for more. Make sure it is done on a cumulative basis not a daily basis.

Choose a Destination

Location, location, location! Remember you are choosing a location that will give your participants the best experience possible. Choose an environment that reinforces your goals and objectives. Your defined purpose will set the tone for your location and site selection.

It is time to choose the right (city and state) for your event — if this is a choice you, the event planner, will be making. Match your site to your event and audience. Make travel easy for your participants. If most of your potential participants are concentrated in one part of the country, hold your meeting in that area, preferably at an easy access gateway, making it easy for attendees to get there. When travelers travel fewer miles, it is also good for the environment.

For participants who will be traveling:

- Where are they coming from?
- How convenient is it for them to travel to this location?
- Does their budget allow for travel to this location?
- How is the weather at this destination during the time of year you have chosen?
- Are there are enough hotels to accommodate the participants?
- Are there enough incoming flights from around the country?
- Is it a desirable destination?
- Are there other attractions around the city?
- Can the participants afford this city?

For participants who are local:

- Is it in a convenient location?
- Is there plenty of parking?
- Is the event space appropriate?

- Is it appropriate for your kind of event?

The destination can be critical. Do you want to have an event in February in Buffalo, New York, or would you attract more participants to Daytona Beach, Florida? Can you imagine choosing Bozeman, Montana, for a conference site for 25,000 attendees? There would not be enough hotel rooms, a conference center large enough, or enough incoming flights.

You get the picture.

Site Selection

When you know the destination, the next task is to select the exact site or venue. In Chapter 3 we listed the vast selection of location-sites to consider when choosing the venue that best suits your defined purpose. You may think you want a hotel because you are accustomed to that type of venue, but the destination you have chosen may have a fabulous, conveniently located university campus with all the necessary amenities and a much cheaper price.

Site selection has never been easier. You are only a click away from finding websites with free global databases containing 40,000-plus meeting and event facilities. These sites are regularly updated with fresh information. They contain extensive photos, meeting room layouts, contacts, and information about the surrounding area.

This is your opportunity to think outside the box and find a unique event space for your event. For assistance in finding out what is available in a city other than your own, contact the convention and visitor's bureau (CVB). They are a valuable resource and will provide information concerning every aspect of the city. They are helpful because their job is to attract business. Not only will they give you a list of all the hotels and facilities in the area, they will help you locate products and services that you may need for your event. Most CVBs have websites where you can request a meeting planners' package.

Cities actively solicit large groups to come to their area because there is so much money in large conventions, conferences and special events. Just think of what cities go through to be in the bidding process for the Olympics. When your destination city does not have a CVB, try the Chamber of Commerce or other planners in the area. Ask local hotels for references and names of planners who have used their venue.

CHOOSE YOUR SITES CAREFULLY

We had been doing our trainings in California at the same site for about four years when we got our first request to perform our weeklong training in Illinois. The group that funded the event chose a university near Evanston as the site. Evanston is a wealthy area, so we went along with the choice thinking it must be a very nice facility. We arrived on the campus very late at night and, until that moment, did not know we were being housed in the freshman dorms. Everyone was housed together, staff, presenters, and all of the 100 participants.

What a nightmare! What I remember are the creaky metal beds, thin tiny towels, no hangers in the closets, and very dusty floors. It was almost like a prison — for an entire week. The participants were not very happy about the accommodations, thinking that we, the staff and faculty, were probably in some nice hotel with room service. When they found out that we were in the same facility, they didn't feel so bad, and we all bonded over the experience in a wonderful way. Fortunately, the cafeteria and meeting rooms turned out to be much nicer.

Moral of this story: Be involved with site selection! After that experience, we became involved in selecting every out-of-state training site. We negotiated with the funders not to sign any contract with any site until we were able to review it or call and confirm that the venue was appropriate for all of our needs and requirements. Even when we did not get the perfect site and all of our needs were not met, we were at least aware of the situation ahead of time and could alert all parties coming to the event.

Karla Nygaard, Conference Coordinator
Sausalito, California

Even though the story above had less than perfect accommodations, universities are still a popular destination. They offer a mix of atmosphere, affordability and services in combination with the advanced technological capabilities needed for the planning and management of events today. They typically offer flexible meeting and event space managed by a team of professionals.

Using convention and visitors bureaus

Convention and visitor bureaus are available in most large cities to provide resources and services to the event planner. They are non-profit organizations specifically formed to represent that city. Their service will save you time by assisting you in selecting the perfect site. It can be a one-stop shop! They can serve as a broker or an official point of contact for event and meeting planners. They are incredibly helpful and at your service.

There are many advantages to using a CVB to assist in planning your event. They are a great resource even if your event is in your local area. They can create collateral material, assist with on-site logistics and registration, provide housing bureau services, develop pre- and post-conference activities such as spouse tours and special events, and help with site inspections and familiarization tours. They can provide speakers and local educational opportunities, help secure special venues, and coordinate local transportation.

CVBs give meeting planners access to a range of services, packages, and value-added extras. They can also link planners with the suppliers, whether it be a motor coach company, a caterer, or an off-site entertainment venue and help meet the prerequisites of any event. Typically, they can help you with events with up to 50,000 participants. Some of the larger bureaus in major cities have staff members dedicated to small events.

Many CVBs will market the destination to attendees with their promotional material, saving you money and encouraging attendance. They will also act as a liaison with community officials, thus clearing the way for special permits, street closures and city requirements. They generate special letters of welcome from high-ranking government officials and in some cases assist in bringing local officials to welcome your participants or well-known entertainers to entertain at your event.

Request for proposal (RFP)

After you have a list of possible sites, write a request for proposal (RFP) to tell the potential site of your needs and request a bid based on your requirements. Include as many aspects of your event that you know, such as the following components:

RFP Information

- Name of the event
- Dates and times (Add alternate dates if you are flexible)
- Date you need a response by
- Your goals and objectives
- Your agenda
- Sleeping room needs – how many and what type (singles, doubles, suites)
- Meeting room needs – how many and what size
- Rates – maximum
- Specific amenities needed – spa, pool, business center, food services, room service, fitness center
- Food and beverage needs
- A-V requirements
- Participant profile (who they are, where they are coming from)

- Number of participants
- History (if this is an annual or regular event)
- Special functions planned on or off the property
- Special dietary needs
- Exhibit space needs
- Support services needed (ADA compliant)
- Non-room space available

Other questions about the facility you should ask:

For Business /Corporate – inside facility

- What is the room tax?
- Are there other groups booked in the hotel on those dates?
- Do you have transportation to/from the airport? What is the cost? How long does it take?
- Do you have a business center? What are the hours?
- Ask for a set of menus and audiovisual cost sheets.
- Do you have an in-house audiovisual department? If not, do you work closely with someone who does? Is there a cost for bringing in an outside company?
- Is the site close to other attractions?
- What is the weather like during our proposed dates?
- Is there plenty of parking? Do you have self-park or valet only? What are the fees?
- Does the facility have a food and beverage department?
- Do you have room service? What are the hours?
- Do you have a fitness center/club? What is the cost? What are the hours?
- Does the facility comply with the ADA (American Disabilities Act)?
- How many sleeping rooms are needed for complimentary rooms?

For Social or Special – outside facility /area

- What other events are happening in the area on those dates?
- Is the site close to other attractions?
- What is the weather like during our proposed dates?
- What kind of parking is there in the neighborhood? Is there specific parking for this venue?
- What types of permits are necessary?
- Will concessions and staging be needed?
- Will we need streets to be closed?
- How secure is the site?
- Is there plenty of parking?
- Is this site accessible by public transportation?

In the RFP, ask for as many amenities as possible. Here is a short list of services you might request: airport transfers, early check-in times, late check-out times, complimentary meeting space, extra storage space, no receiving charges, continental breakfast in the meeting rooms, extended-stay rates, free local calls, free office space, free or reduced parking for VIPs and staff, health club access, late cutoff dates, reduced room rates for staff and speakers, upgrades for VIPs and staff, welcome gifts and notes, electrical fee reduction, discounted exhibit space, just to name a few. Do not be afraid to ask. All they can do is say yes or no.

Site Inspections

Do a physical site inspection when possible. Absolutely do the inspection when your event is local. When you travel to another city or state for the inspections, try to visit several sites during one trip. Brochures and websites usually enhance or show only the best side of a site. Site inspections allow you to confirm the information provided about a property and evaluate it personally and meet the personnel. See for yourself whether the site meets your criteria. Remember, a hotel will usually give you a complimentary night or two during your stay if the site is out of your town. They should offer.

If not, ask! Do a visual walkthrough of your event before you do your site inspection to determine space requirements. You might need a 20-foot ceiling for staging and audiovisual equipment. Will you need dressing rooms for entertainers, office space for your staff, an exhibit area? Will you need loading docks, large parking areas, portable rest rooms, cooking facilities? What equipment will you need to have delivered?

Prearrange a meeting with the hotel department heads: the general manager, sales manager, catering manager, and the technical manager. Also take the opportunity to meet the front desk staff, banquet servers, bell captains, and concierge — the people who will directly interact with your participants. Watch the staff in their daily operations. Do they have the qualities you want? Are they accommodating, calm, helpful, friendly, professional and prompt? Do they a deliver a consistently high level of service?

Evaluate every aspect of the hotel or venue — the sleeping rooms, meeting rooms, lobby, restaurants, recreational areas, parking, and accessibility to all parts of the venue that your guests will be using. Observe areas that will directly affect the production end of the event. Do a walkthrough and inspect the loading docks, receiving departments, a/v and banquet equipment, dimension restrictions for delivery vehicles, loading/unloading equipment, or electrical/lighting options. Take note whether the site has restrictions, zoning regulations or noise restrictions.

Evaluate the exact condition of the venue cleanliness, décor and quality of the exterior of the building as well as the interiors including the furniture, paint and carpets. Ask whether any construction or restoration will be taking place during the dates of your event.

Walk around the neighborhood. Check the distance and ease of transfer from airports and freeways. Is there accessibility to other area attractions? Eat in their restaurants, evaluate the quality and variety of the food, confirm that the banquet food is the same quality, see other banquet displays, and witness the level of service in serving staff. Take copious notes while you do your site inspection. They will come in handy if you visit several sites in one or two days. Or use the video camera on your smartphone to record your site inspections so that you remember the property.

KNOW YOUR NEIGHBORS - MULTIPLE DAY SEMINARS

Attendees: 100 Educators

At a beautiful hotel and resort in San Diego, we neglected to ask who else would be using the hotel during our multiple day seminars. It was a popular hotel on a bay, a stylish venue with weddings throughout the year. A large wedding was taking place during our event with hundreds of people. The ceremony was conducted directly outside one of our meeting rooms. After the wedding concluded and their reception began — guess what — they had a loud band and it was right next door to our evening meeting room.

Both events were disruptive to our meetings. Be sure to check with the hotel, and ask who your neighbors might be.

Karla Nygaard, Conference Coordinator
Sausalito, California

Outdoor Sites

Site inspections for outdoor events are extremely critical. The issues and challenges are vastly different from producing an event in a contained facility such as a hotel or convention center. Using public streets, parks, and public or private buildings can be a logistical headache even for the most experienced planners. For outdoor extravaganzas, many people and services are required, and the tasks are diverse, large and complicated. Specialists in different areas should be brought in to make your event run smoothly. With outside events there will always be last-minute challenges. They are inevitable. Be prepared.

Timing is essential for outdoor productions. Many of these events are on public streets, and you might find that the time limit can be tight. When you are closing off streets and controlling crowds, you may only have an eight-hour setup window for a huge public event with thousands of attendees. It may be that streets cannot be cleared for access until businesses close for the night. You may need to get in quick and get out fast. Some of the questions you might encounter when organizing an outside event are:

- What is the power supply source?
- Where will we put the stage?
- What kind of permits will we need?
- What kind of insurance will we need?
- Do we need to get city police and fire departments involved?
- Will we need our own security?
- Where should we set up food concessions?
- How much time do we have for setup and takedown?
- Who owns the property?
- What is the weather for that time of year?

MANAGING YOUR TRASH

When you have large outside events with thousands of people, expect to generate a mountain of trash. Here is a story about how the planners of San Francisco's weekend-long Pride Celebration built a model for trash control and recycling. Because of the success of the program, the City of San Francisco has used this model for their large events since then.

The Pride Parade draws half a million participants to its June festivities. The event's large public venue is a one-and-a-half-mile parade route and 14-square-block celebration area. Two of the biggest logistical challenges have always been managing crowds and managing their trash. To help revelers stow their trash properly, four on-site recycling stations were manned by pros that told participants about the benefits of recycling and pointed out what is recyclable and what is not. The recycling system involves blue, green, and black bins for different kinds of reusable waste and is incorporated throughout the huge event site. When it comes to recycling, San Francisco is one of the leaders.

Angela Wrigley
San Francisco Pride Volunteer

You can expect to be working with different services and vendors than you would be in a contained facility. Some of the purveyors you might encounter are the city, county, state, food vendors, lighting and technical professionals, security firms, sign makers, caterers and kitchen facilities, portable rest room companies, rental equipment, companies for equipment and supplies such as portable heaters or electricity, fences, bleachers, ticket booths, exhibits booths, barricades, tables and chairs, linens and tableware, tenting, and staging. And more!

Good vendor relationships are key to producing great festivals. If you are using a vendor or service for the first time, get bids from several suppliers. Stick with experienced vendors who have become familiar with the event's specific needs. Get recommendations whenever possible.

The ADA

The Americans with Disabilities Act (ADA) laws are strict and require organizers to take into consideration many important characteristics for every meeting and event. Work together with a facility so that you are in compliance. Even though it is the responsibility of the facility to provide accessibility, it is your responsibility to ensure they do so.

When creating marketing material, have space on your registration and hotel reservation forms where participants can indicate a need for special accommodations. It is your responsibility to make space on the registration form, and it will be the facility's responsibility to contact those who checked the box to determine specific needs for the room accommodations. It is against ADA laws to require that the person with the disability contact the organization or facility to expand upon their needs. This would require disabled attendees to do something non-disabled attendees do not have to do, which goes against the ADA.

A hearing-impaired guest may only require seating in the front row to read the speaker's lips if they do not have expensive special equipment. Similarly, a sight-impaired attendee may not need Braille materials because it is likely they already own the equipment necessary to enable them to participate in the program. They may only need assistance getting around the meeting or permission to have a guide dog present. A specially built registration counter to accommodate those in wheelchairs is not necessary. Simply making a clipboard available so that a wheelchair-bound attendee can fill out registration forms will suffice.

ADA laws require that individuals with disabilities inform the organization of special accommodations in advance. If they do not, the organization is not bound by ADA laws to accommodate their needs. That does not mean you will not go to any lengths to do so when appropriate.

Accommodating participants with disabilities does not have to be a challenge. Set up session and function rooms with wider aisles, or remove seating to allow for wheelchairs. Doing so may affect the room set-up and capacities. Be sure to have adequate ramps if attendees or speakers will be on stage. Knowing the ADA facts and figures is important. Make sure all aspects of the facility are in compliance with ADA laws, including:

- Public areas
- Alarm systems
- Front desk
- Door widths
- Barrier free
- Elevator button height-adapted guest rooms (inside and out)
- Hallways

Type of Event: Performance
Duration: Two hours
Number of Attendees: 300
Type of Venue: Small Theater with three banks of seats/two aisles

Subject of Story: Accommodating individuals with conflicting needs, I serve on the board of Culture! Disability! Talent! It is a disability arts organization. I was asked to be one of several ushers for a performance featuring four of our members. As part of event publicity, we included a standard invitation for people to request accommodations and a request of our own that attendees not wear perfume or scented products.

Immediately after we had seated a ticket holder with a guide dog in the center bank of seats, another ticket holder informed us that she was severely allergic to dogs. We had an obligation to make sure her risk of an allergic reaction was minimized, but we had an equal obligation not to deny the guide dog owner her right to her primary means of navigation.

Solution: We talked to the allergic woman for a few minutes about options and decided to declare the right bank of seats the "dog zone" and the left bank the "dog-free zone." We asked the guide dog owner to move to the right bank, which she did without complaint. As more people with dogs entered the theater, we steered them toward the right bank of seats, explaining why. We also made an announcement before the performance started so that people who wished to avoid the dogs could move to the left bank of seats. This appeared to be satisfactory to everyone, including the original person with the allergy.

Lesson: While not all issues involving two or more people with disabilities who have conflicting needs can be resolved this easily, it's always worth taking some time to find out details on what everyone needs as an accommodation and propose appropriate solutions.

Jane Berliss-Vincent, Director, Adult/Senior Services
Berkeley, California, **www.cforat.org**

Using a Destination Management Company

Going into a city for the first time and planning an event using unknown vendors and services can be overwhelming. Although the Internet, guides, and Web pages are a good start, there is a breed of companies that have come to the rescue: destination management companies (DMC).

You may need assistance with logistics. There are good resources, such as other event planners, but it is best to talk with a team of authentic local people in the industry. This is where the DMCs can be incredibly helpful. They make it easier to work with one vendor rather than dozens of different providers. Just how many catering companies will you want to talk with before finding the right one? The same goes for the audiovisual, technical equipment, transportation, and security companies. One point of contact is a great benefit. As a planner, you deal with hundreds of details so that using a good DMC can increase your bottom line.

Are they worth the money and time? With the Internet, do you need a middleman? This is a valid question! A DMC has valuable local knowledge so that they can provide logistical support, local hotel backgrounds, audiovisual services, transportation schedules, and catering possibilities. It may be worth the cost.

Choosing Talent

The best sources of available speakers or entertainers are referrals from colleagues and friends. Get recommendations first. If your personal resources are not accessible, try a speakers' bureau to find and book the best possible choice for your needs depending on your budget and requirements. The Internet is a great resource. You can also find some suggestions in the *Reference* section of this book or check professional organizations.

Speaker/lecturer/instructor

The right speaker or entertainment can make or break your event. Choose an expert when appropriate, someone who is motivational, captivating, well-known in your business or just plain entertaining. Choose someone who is reliable and recognizable or someone who has something new to offer your group. Will your group benefit from a sports celebrity, a best-selling author, a television personality, a well-known industry insider, or someone from within your own group?

In your planning sessions, you would have decided the topic for speakers. Some events are even built around the speaker's availability, which determines dates and location. Choosing keynote and final speakers is incredibly important to draw in your participants. Make sure your speakers are interesting, motivated, lively, funny and knowledgeable. The speakers and instructors you select, be they professional trainers, volunteers or senior management, will play a large part in determining whether you will reach your goals. Ask about their presentation and their style of speaking. Ensure that they are a good fit for your audience. After you have chosen your speakers, provide them with information and guidance about your organization, and share your expectations of their presentations.

After you have chosen the right individual for your program, generate a contract to state your expectations, and confirm exactly what you are offering the person. (See a sample letter in the *Reference* section.) Be sure to include your request to view their presentation in advance of the event. You might need to incorporate the material into your marketing material.

Find our early what their requirements are for audio-visual and communication needs. They many need a Wi-Fi connection for their presentation or just a microphone. It is good to know since audiovisual and technology equipment can be expensive, especially if ordered last-minute.

Entertainers

For entertainment, match the music and the talent to the theme of your party and your participants. A cello quartet at a 10-year high school class reunion might be inappropriate, but it could be well-suited to your parents' 50th wedding anniversary.

Certain events will require adding entertainment — even celebrities. You can locate entertainers by word-of-mouth, on the Internet, or from a recommendation from another meeting professional. Check your budget first because speakers, entertainers and celebrities cost money. It is common to have multiple entertainers at one event, such as a pianist for cocktail hours, a band for dancing after dinner, or several entertainers in various rooms simultaneously.

The speakers' budget

Speaker fees are subjective. You should always make an offer. A speaker can charge $5,000 and easily be worth much more, or you might pay $15,000 and be greatly disappointed. How realistic is it to think you can get that $25,000 speaker to do a date for less? It is possible. Here are some effective strategies you can try.

Ask the speaker to give the initial speech and perhaps participate on a panel in another session, attend the reception to greet the guests, or sit at a round table discussion. After you have them in your corner, ask them to participate in other ways that are not too imposing. You would be surprised at those who are willing to do more. Do not forget to ask them to play a round of golf with some of the high-level members of your sales team or executives. They can always say no, but then, think of the excitement when they say yes!

If you have multiple meetings in multiple cities and one speaker is relevant to all events, try booking the person for a series of meetings. Given the opportunity to relay the same message to multiple audiences, the speaker may reduce his or her fee.

The Learning Annex, for example, has thousands of trainers, teachers and best-selling authors available on a daily basis around the country. Why not tap into one of their programs? Instead of having the speaker or expert come to your event, take your participants to them. Some of their exceptional seminars bring several popular speakers together and can be purchased for as little as $69 per participant for an all-day event. Take advantage of these pre-arranged, fairly priced opportunities and get much more for your dollar. (And leave the planning to them!)

For Entertainers fees, which are also subjective, try the above suggestions.

Signing a contract

Your speaker or entertainer should sign a contract, either his own document or one that you provide. There is a sample contract in the Appendix. A professional will typically request more amenities as part of performing at your event, such as first-class airfare for herself and her assistants, a suite at a hotel, limos to and from the airport, specific foods, flowers, special drinks, and travel pay to and from the site.

MONEY SAVING TIPS

➤ Choose speakers who can also be workshop leaders.

➤ Find someone local to save on travel expenses.

➤ Negotiate the speakers' fees. Offer a flat amount rather than a fee and all expenses.

➤ Offer the speaking session as a chance for the speaker to update videos or record them for their podcast or webinar. These expenses paid by the speaker could run into the thousands.

➤ To save on speaker expenses, consider using industry experts whose companies often pay expenses. Check how good they are before hiring them. You may end up with a dud!

➤ If dates are flexible, plan meetings around the speaker's schedule, and piggyback the trip with other speaking engagements.

➤ If speakers have books or products to sell, consider buying them for the participants in lieu of speakers' fees.

➤ Pay with in-kind contributions instead of cash. For example, allow them the opportunity to sell their products, or offer them exposure to their market.

Create the Agenda

Every event has a beginning, middle and end. Each step of the process needs to be defined clearly. An agenda is the schedule for the day's activities laid out in time increments. It is your tool for getting the right information to the right people. The agenda will tell them where to be, what to expect when they get there, what to do at what time, and for how long.

There are two types of agendas. One is for the participants coming to a business or educational meeting. It is a road map for the day's schedule informing them where to go, what will be taking place, how long it will last, and when to take breaks, meet for meals, or have free time.

The other is for volunteers, staff, vendors, planners and those working behind the scenes. This agenda is for any event. It is a timeline schedule with the duties, tasks, times and responsibilities for specific assistants or volunteers. It might say, "Caterer arrives at 10 a.m. for beginning preparation. Florist will arrive at 10:30 a.m. with 50 bouquets of tabletop rounds. Tables and chairs arrive at 10:45 a.m., and the delivery of champagne is due at 11 a.m. Valerie will be on hand to sign for all of the above deliveries.

Business and educational agendas

Create your agenda to support your defined purpose. The better you are acquainted with your attendees, the more thorough your agenda will be and the more satisfied they will be. Consider the reason they are meeting and what you are going to give them, and then give them what they came for. Do this by choosing the right speakers or entertainers, covering the appropriate topics, and giving them plenty of time to absorb the information. Make sure there are breaks and time for networking, and bring them together for meals or other social events.

If they came to learn about a new product, introduce the product. If they came for fun, make sure your agenda includes fun. If they came to conduct business, incorporate meetings into your agenda. If they came to be educated, teach them. Your agenda should cover all the promised topics in a timely fashion that works for the greater good.

Do a mockup of the entire agenda. Make sure to include adequate time for registration, meals, breaks, speakers, awards, down time and socializing. Do a visual run-through of the event and make notes of how you see it happening. Run this by your team, and confirm that it works.

TIPS ON AGENDA PREPARATION

Today we are overflowing with information. Our knowledge is doubling yearly and accelerating. We can now access a world of data 24/7/365. Our minds are trying to comprehend thousands of bits of material as we are barraged with advertising, emails, commercials, social media, texts, and on and on. Multitasking is the new norm, and we are being overwhelmed.

Our attention spans are decreasing because of this bombardment. So take note when setting up your agendas to keep your audience awake and alert. Here are some suggestions:
- Get your participants more involved through activity or tools.
- Get them out of their chairs for networking, quick exercises, role playing or games.
- Create shorter presentation times.
- Use images, short videos.
- Keep the pace of the presentation lively.

Be prepared for last-minute agenda changes. They may be significant, requiring you to transform the event to meet a different purpose. Even a small, unexpected occurrence can jolt you into an immediate change in plans. The following experience shows how the event producers quickly made the appropriate modifications to fit in the allotted time schedule.

Type of Event: Corporate Meeting/Event
Duration: Half-Day session with working lunch – presentations; group exercises/ brainstorming sessions over lunch
Number of Attendees: 350 people
Type of Venue: Hotel conference center (large gathering rooms and smaller meeting rooms)
Subject of Story: Late change in plans.

I was working with a senior technology manager and her team on plans for a department-wide planning session. We had two main goals:

1) Provide an interesting, informative series of presentations for the technology staff on business purpose and technology plans for the future.
2) Provide a venue where participants could break into smaller groups to tackle ideas, questions, and issues in small brainstorming sessions and then come together to share the results.

A week before the session, the company announced plans for Take Your Child to Work Day. The day of the planning session was identified as a primary day for children to accompany their parents to work.

Problem: The event was the antithesis of a child-oriented day. It would be boring for the children, and it was likely that the children would distract the adults, yet explicitly excluding children would send the wrong message.

Solution: We needed to embrace the concept of accommodating children as though it were another requirement of the project. I knew that the best alternative would be one that removed them from the proceedings to everyone's advantage.

I proposed an off-site planning session for children. They would spend the first 30 minutes with the adults during the welcome session. Then they would be escorted out to their own creative, fun-filled day! An advance invitation to adult participants, with another invitation specifically for children, would ensure that everyone was clear on the day's program. The proposal was accepted. I would be working with the adults, and I needed someone to work with the children.

On very short notice, I called two associates (one of them Shannon!) and asked, begged, pleaded, implored and beseeched them for help!

About 40 children accompanied their parents to the event. They attended the welcome session and were then escorted out to their own off-site meeting. There they worked in teams to brainstorm how we would all use technology in the future for monetary transactions. Each team designed and developed a presentation. Then, the children returned to the adult session where each team delivered their presentation. The event was a win-win for everyone. The children were beaming as they accepted their recognition certificates. We were rated excellent in the feedback.

Lesson learned:
➡ Some opportunities masquerade as problems.
➡ Contain a problem, but also try to see how it can work to your advantage.
➡ Children are extraordinarily imaginative. (I'm convinced some of them have gone on to be engineers!)

Susan Mason
Mason and Wall Communications

MONEY SAVING TIPS

➡ Evaluate the number of breakout sessions. By reducing them you can save food and beverage costs, speakers' fees, audiovisual costs, and room rental fees.
➡ Book all speakers' presentations for the same room if they have the same audiovisual and technology needs.

Social and special events agendas

Timing for social and special events is very critical. Set-up can be time-consuming. Consider stages, lighting, tenting, tables, chairs, booths, signs, electricity, barricades, and other specific equipment. It can be demanding because there is often a short time to get the stage set. Dozens of vendors, volunteers and staff may arrive about the same time and will be coming and going frequently. It is imperative that someone is in charge of verifying the arrival of these people, giving the correct directions to them and confirming that they are equipped to do their jobs.

The agenda for these events may be down to the minute, listing who is in charge, exactly what is happening, where it is happening, and who is coming or going. There could be several schedules for an event that may last only two hours. You will have a list for catering people, transportation companies, registration team, decorators and designers. The head coordinator will be in charge of all the staff leaders working each area. There may be hundreds of volunteers requiring several leaders to assign and direct suppliers and vendors.

Hundreds of things can be going on simultaneously, and the more that is written down and confirmed, the better off everyone will be. You will know exactly when the bakery truck is arriving, the exact quantities they are to deliver, and who will meet them and sign for the delivery. As you can see, these agendas are powerful. They can save the day if one key person is absent because you can hand off the schedule to someone else to pick up and run that responsibility.

Add wellness to your agenda

Because mind and body are connected, when you experience tension, fatigue and tightness in the body, you also feel it in the mind. Moving the body relieves and creates more space for the mind to internalize.

Research shows that starting the day with movement and exercise is one of the key elements for people to get energized as well as be alert and focused.

- At multi-day meetings, an opportunity to add movement to the agenda will help stimulate the brain and body, to bring oxygen into the body is great for brain function. So do the hokey pokey!
- Sometimes getting people to get up earlier on an already long day may be difficult. Perhaps offer a prize or other incentive.
- Get speakers to take movement breaks as well. Every 20 minutes, get up and exercise, have the participant use their chairs for stretches or knee bends and every 45 minutes to get up and move around the room. Make it fun!
- Also begin meeting with three minutes of exercise as it helps retain new information.
- Get outdoors if possible.

CHAPTER

12

Creating Atmosphere

Creating an atmosphere that will keep your participants comfortable, well cared-for, secure, and satisfied should be one your top priorities. Customer satisfaction is elevated when the participants are getting what they came for and more.

If they came to meet the new board members or sponsors, introduce them and have them mingle with the participants. If they came to learn new techniques, teach them! If they came to have fun, give it to them! Make them comfortable while they are there. When you do this, your participants will walk away from your event fulfilled. When the customer is satisfied, you have a successful event!

Customer satisfaction means setting up the venue so that maneuvering is easy, the audiovisual systems are well-arranged, access to registrations, tickets and materials is simple, and food and drink is plentiful. You will need to make the surroundings comfortable and conducive to the ongoing activities. You will also need to feed participants and equip them with all the materials needed to fulfill their reasons for coming. The result is that you will be guaranteed a good reputation and valuable word-of-mouth publicity.

Technology plays a large role in creating your atmosphere. Using the newest equipment is so important that we have an entire chapter in this guide called *Staying on Top of Technology*. Look there for the most up-to-date electronic and audiovisual equipment as well as computer and Internet paraphernalia. In this chapter, we look at the reasons your event may require equipment, something that will help determine the venue.

Room Set-Up and Designs

Turning a typical meeting space into a learning environment is about more than arranging chairs and tables in classroom style. Room set-up, lighting, sound, temperature, supplies and amenities are critical to successful learning.

Room set-up can mean the difference between success and failure. If the participants are uncomfortable, they will remember that above all else. Make sure the room is set up to be beneficial to the event you are producing.

People learn more when they interact with other people. A session that allows for networking among peers is often more valuable than just one or two speakers talking to an audience all day. A room that allows for movement and networking is important. You should face your audience toward the long wall in any room to expose more people to the front/stage area, especially important if you have a long, narrow room. Consider the direction from which people are entering the room. Have them enter from the back. Do not have people entering from the front while the speaker or entertainer is talking, or you will have constant interruptions and embarrassed latecomers.

Try to visit the room before deciding on a room setup so that you have first-hand knowledge of how the room will work for you, the participants and the speakers. Find out if there is another event scheduled in the room before yours is to begin. Know what time they will finish so that you have enough time to check the room before your event begins. Also find out if there are other events going on next to your room, and make sure that the walls will filter out their noise.

The typical room layouts seen in the diagrams below are still commonly used and work well when you take into consideration the objectives of the event. Look at the following overviews to determine the best layout design for your function.

Classroom Style: This layout is best suited when participants will be taking notes, using a computer, or referring to material of some kind. This is not a great setup when you want a lot of networking. It is typically used for a longer session and when the presenter will be doing most of the talking.

Hollow Square or Rectangle Style: This setup is nice for educational sessions, large committee meetings, board of directors meetings or staff meetings.

Theatre Style: Best use here is when maximum seating capacity is needed. This design is used when speakers are on stage and/or they will be showing presentations. Not practical when attendees must take notes.

Banquet Style: This style is typically used for meal functions. It is also good for small breakouts or committees where networking and note-taking are required.

Conference Style: Used for board or committee meetings where interaction will be anticipated. This can also be good for food and beverage functions for small gatherings.

U-shape Style: Good for board and committee meetings and break-out session. Good for meetings that involve A-V presentations. This style can serve for banquets as well.

Always work with the banquet department of the venue because they will know the best arrangement for each of their rooms. You will need to be specific in your instructions and needs.

BAD STAGE DESIGN

During a meeting, a speaker was at the podium onstage. To the side of the podium were a table and chairs. Being a motivational speaker, he moved around as he spoke and would rest his hands on the chair. Each time the chair moved ever so slightly until one leg slipped off the stage unnoticed. The next time he rested his hands on it, the chair tumbled off the stage, and he followed. Fortunately, he was not hurt. He popped up quickly and was back on stage in a flash continuing his presentation.

Anonymous

MONEY SAVING TIPS

➡ Wherever possible, use theater style (where only chairs are used).

➡ It is less labor-intensive than classroom-style (which includes both table and chairs), thus lowering setup costs. Also, plan to keep setups the same from day to day.

➡ Cut down on classroom-style set-ups for some of the rooms. They require more labor, more space, and are slower to turn into another setting compared to theater style.

➡ Work with groups in the venue before and after your event. Try sharing room set-up and maybe even speakers and audiovisual equipment.

➡ Use the same room with two setups. For example, use the room class-room-style for the course and banquet-style for lunch and breaks. Put up screens or use plants to divide the space.

Registration and ticket sales area

Your participants' first encounter with the event will be the registration tables or ticket counter. Make sure this area runs smoothly. If it does not, you appear disorganized and unprepared. Work with the venue to come up with the best possible scenario for the number of people you are expecting.

The layout of your registration area is a vital consideration. It will be a focal point. When laying out this area, pretend you are an attendee and walk through the process. Make it easy and quick, and avoid long lines whenever possible. If they have to complete the registration onsite, make it easy to complete the form. You might want to use computer kiosks with online registration. When setting up the layout, consider the following points:

• Is the registration/ticket sales area located in a central place?

- Which direction will people enter from?
- Can they see the signs?
- Is there enough room for lines of people?
- Can people with disabilities easily register?
- Is there a place attendees can go if they have questions or need time to fill out forms? A help desk?
- Can attendees pick up their materials from any of the registration staff or must they go to another table or booth?
- Do you need a special registration area for exhibitors, VIPs, speakers or sponsors?
- Will you have on-site registration for those who did not register early?
- Do you need to collect payment?
- Do you need a phone line for credit card verification?
- Will you need Internet access?
- Do you need tables for displays, pamphlets or handouts?
- Do you need tables for vendors?

Audiovisual Choices

Most events will require audiovisual equipment of some sort. There is a chapter later in this book devoted to technology with emphasis on audiovisual equipment. See the chapter on *Technologically Speaking*. The days of the slide projectors, overhead projectors and microphones are gone. Today, the industry is technically sophisticated, and you may require training or an audiovisual tech to become your best friend.

Because of the sophistication of technology today, make sure to order only the absolute necessities because this stuff is not cheap. When done well, it will enhance your event. Done poorly it is a distraction. And you, the coordinator, will have to deal with it and usually at the last minute.

Today's speakers, entertainers and event participants expect the latest technology: computerized presentations, wide screens for extra-large rooms or simulcast into additional rooms, Internet access, satellite downlinks, and video conferencing to name a few. Confirm with your speakers and entertainers exactly what their needs are for their presentations.

Discuss with both the venue and the audiovisual company your needs, and confirm that they are in the position to meet your standards and requirements. Ask them for testimonials, or discuss what sets them apart from other companies. Ask if they have any specialized services, like state-of-the-art technology in lighting, sound, staging or rigging. And make sure you budget for all of it.

Whether you use your venue's service or an outside company, ensure they are equipped to handle any unexpected changes such as replacement equipment or last-minute additions. Will they have extra equipment on-site, or are they connected to an outside company that will respond immediately? Find out how long the technical staff has been with the facility, and know how familiar they are with the venue staff and the facility itself. Involve them in all of the pre-event meetings so that they are current with any and all changes.

The audiovisual company you hire should be properly insured. The contract should include the insurance requirements. In particular, the company should carry at least $2 million in liability insurance coverage and workers' compensation insurance. Ask them to provide you with proof (a certificate) of their liability insurance coverage. Depending on your event and whether you have your own insurance, you may request that you and your clients are listed as insured on their policy, providing you with extra insurance coverage.

Access to Wi-Fi

Your participants will expect high-speed Internet access while they are attending your function, especially if it keeps them away from the office for more than a day. We are conditioned to stay in touch with our work, our families and our daily Internet habits. The biggest problem for you, the planner, or the organization is budget. Can you afford it?

The use of kiosks at outdoor events is just as common as finding public computers in hotels and convention centers. At a high profile triathlon in San Francisco, there were at least 15 stand-alone computers for participants, spectators or anyone passing by to add comments, give feedback, take surveys and print coupons. They were paid for by the sponsor of the event, but within the applications on the computer, other exhibitors had the opportunity to advertise their products as well.

Take these ideas into consideration when figuring out what your venue can offer and if it is adequate for your participants' needs. Have a good idea what the high-speed access will be used for since all applications are not the same. If participants simply want to check their email throughout the event, one system can be used. However, if you require many uses, such as video conferencing, web streaming or instant messaging, a different system will be needed altogether. Find out what your speakers and workshop leaders will need and tie that in with what the participants expect.

Check with the venue to see what type of Internet security system they have. They may have a firewall that would inhibit the use of many types of communications. At the same time, find out what type of service the venue currently has. Who is their provider, and what kind of technical support do they have on-site or on contract? How quickly can they respond to technical difficulties? Is an on-site technician required?

Some service providers will simply install the system without support while others give ongoing support to the contract's end. Take advantage of the venue's technical support contract if there is one. Sometimes, the venue will have technical support on staff. Whatever the case may be, know what is offered before signing a contract or choosing that particular venue.

Budgeting your Internet access

Compare pricing when planning this amenity. If the venue has a provider, you probably will have to use them. If not, get bids from several businesses. Prices will vary for the different services you will want or need. You can be charged for different types of connections and for the number of computers you will use. Plan on paying one fee for the original connection, a fee per computer, and then a possible fee per computer connection.

Should you charge for the connection? Attendees will likely expect Internet and Wi-Fi connection to be free. Here is your opportunity to use sponsorship dollars. You might be able to offset some of the expenses by charging a few more dollars in the registration fee. If you choose to have the computers at no cost to your attendees, put that information in your marketing material. You can make it a win-win-win situation: give the participants what they want, offer a great opportunity for a sponsor, and look great by providing this terrific resource.

Audiovisual considerations

- If you are in the early stages of identifying your audiovisual needs, prepare a request for proposal with your requirements, and get at least two bids. Get the bids even if you know you will use the in-house company to give yourself an idea of costs that you can use as leverage with the in-house company. Make sure you know the cost of equipment, labor and service fees as well as how taxes are calculated.
- Consider signing a contract early with the audiovisual company to lock in rates.
- Several weeks before your meeting (before you order any audiovisual equipment), get the name of the in-house audiovisual manager, and call to introduce yourself. Find out the name and contact information of the individual you will be working with on-site, and make sure all of your audiovisual requirements go through that person.
- Provide a diagram. Get a floor plan of your meeting room directly from the venue. Sketch in your preferences for setting up the room. Then work with the audiovisual staff.
- Let the audiovisual company know your budget, and ask them to work with you. When they know your goals and your budget, they will be better equipped to fulfill your needs.

Technical support

Be sure to have good technical support on-site! There is nothing more frustrating than a piece of equipment that breaks down at a crucial moment. Be sure to check all equipment before the event starts. Some venues will charge extra for this service, but it is well worth the money.

MONEY SAVING TIPS

➥ Look outside the hotel for possible audiovisual suppliers whose prices may be more competitive. However, the venue may match the other supplier's prices if asked.

➥ If you have both general session and breakout rooms, try to use the general session room as one of your breakouts to save on audiovisual costs.

➥ When on-site, consider purchasing laser pointers, flip charts and easels. Many times, a single day's cost of renting these items equals the purchase price! Plus, buy spares, and you can give the laser pointers away as gifts for the speakers.

➥ Limit the number of microphones needed. Check whether the hotel supplies a complimentary microphone in each meeting room. Skirt a cocktail table instead of renting special carts for A-V equipment.

➥ Limit use of wireless microphones.

➥ Use one microphone for two speakers.

➥ Re-confirm speakers' audiovisual needs. Avoid ordering more equipment than necessary.

➥ Bring your own equipment.

Program Material and Promotional Gifts

We all enjoy receiving a gift. Event materials and mementos come in all different shapes and sizes. There are conference packets, name tags, programs, handouts, ribbons, giveaways (coffee mugs, T-shirts with logos), certificates, and a tote bag to carry them all in. Leaving with more stuff than you came with has become a tradition. Promotional items for a sports event will differ greatly from what is given at a corporate team-building seminar.

Whatever you want to give away, it must be in line with your defined purpose. But also keep in mind your environmental standards. A gift may not be appropriate unless it is within the guidelines and meets your standards. The choice of your gift will be a part of your goals and objectives and will depend on your budget. It is a great form of publicity and marketing that can keep on working well after your event is over.

At a conference, name tags are a must, but they are not necessary at the town's May Day parade or a wedding. However, a program of the parade would be nice and T-shirts with the logo and dates could be relevant. A special keepsake for a wedding is traditional, showing the name of the couple and their wedding date. You are only limited by your imagination and budget as to what you can offer your attendees. If something has worked in the past, keep the item but jazz it up a bit, or change it slightly and give it a new twist.

Gifts

A little extra effort, creativity and expense can go a long way in getting the attention of the participants and making them feel special. Depending on the event itself, a gift is important or appropriate. If the gift is a reminder of an enjoyable event and your gracious hospitality, your logo is emblazed on the item, and it will be used and seen for years to come, that is a great marketing device!

Decide whether the promotional items should be useful or memorable before you choose them. They must be suitable, useful, thoughtful, imaginative, relevant, and increase name recognition. Do not just pick something to have something. People have diverse tastes and styles. One size does not fit all. Choose something with mass appeal, and make it work for you! Are you carrying a canvas bag or using a pen, money clip, or paper weight on your desk that has a company logo from an event you attended?

Do not give them a throwaway souvenir. Stick to something they will really love, like an iTunes gift card or organic, fair-trade chocolates, or think of something unique such as planting trees in their names at your local park or calculating the amount of money to donate to one of the zero emission companies to offset travel. If your event is appropriate, have the supplier actually on site.

Keep in mind shipping costs to get your gifts to the site, and be sure to put it in the budget.

Food and Beverage Choices

There is a very strong connection between the food served and the overall sentiment of the participants' experience of the event. So it is important to get it right.

Planning for food and beverage at your events can be complicated and time-consuming, but the good news is that most hotels, caterers and restaurants will work closely with you to plan the perfect menu choices. They have great suggestions and recommendations that will assist you in creating menus. They will know what is in season and what would be best served on your particular dates. And since they are experts, they can easily work within your budget. Ultimately, it is your job to research all of your options.

Knowledge of your audience is important before creating your menus. It is critical to offer participants food and drinks that will enhance their ability to learn and pay attention versus something that might spike energy levels or induce drowsiness. What is the difference between a "pick-me-up" and a "space-me-out" afternoon snack?

Trends come and go. Keep up to date on what is popular and desired by your participants. Average people are more sophisticated about food today due to the popularity of shows like "Master Chef" and other food shows on the Food Network channels. Health issues are also in the news, and people are more interested in eating right than ever before. They are health-conscience about foods they want to eat.

Food will be one of your biggest expenses whether you are sitting down to a full-course dinner, serving coffee and snacks for a couple days of morning and afternoon breaks, hiring outside vendors to set up shop at your event, or just having a cocktail reception. Know how much you can spend, and create your menus accordingly. We offer many cost-cutting suggestions that will provide your participants with quality food and beverages.

The liabilities of serving alcohol are of great concern today. The only way to eliminate liquor liability is to eliminate alcohol from your event, but if that is not an option, you can take steps to keep your attendees from overindulging and decreasing your liability.

Know Your Audience

Take into consideration the age, nationality, gender, religion and special meal circumstances of your participants. Some may require low-carbohydrate, low-sodium, high-protein, low-fat, no sugar, kosher, or vegetarian dishes. Some may have food allergies. Make sure you put these choices in your registration forms so your participants can pre-order these selections.

There will always be a group that loves their meat and potatoes, but there are those with diverse tastes who want sashimi tuna pierced on forks displayed handles down, a quick grab shrimp hanging from tree branches, stuffed lobster tail, or a buffet station where wait staff is dressed in themed costumes serving tastes of warm liquid Belgian chocolate over some decadent imported vanilla cookies. That is why knowing your audience is key to ordering the appropriate meal. A meal that would be appropriate for the National Cattlemen's Association could be wrong for a Fortune 500 CEO retirement party.

Work with your caterer or chef to design meals around whatever your food choices for your specific members might be. If you are planning an outdoor festival for Cinco de Mayo, you'd be sure to invite food vendors that made Mexican food and that meet the other requirements for your theme. You would do the same for a sit-down dinner with your company or a breakfast for the local chamber of commerce. Each menu will be different depending on who is sitting at the table.

At a four-day conference in Berkeley, California, a complimentary breakfast was offered to a certain portion of the group. Being free, the 110-seat capacity filled up quickly. The budget was tight, but we were able to provide a good selection of breakfast items. The participants were 95 percent women. Immediately, complaints starting coming in: "Where's the protein?" they demanded. Yes, they were quite vocal about the lack of protein. I quickly contacted the banquet manager on site and asked what we could serve quickly that could fill the void. She informed me that the least expensive choice would be hard-boiled eggs but would take about 15 minutes to arrive. I said do it and quickly went back to the area to inform the participants what was coming. This incident was talked about for the rest of the conference. Who knew that there would be such a harsh complaint for a free breakfast? Know who you are dealing with, and try to cover your bases.

Kyla K.
San Diego, California

Trends Come and Go

What is trendy today may not be next year or the year after that. Our taste in food and our knowledge about food changes constantly. Food fashion waxes and wanes. Most chefs can step up with the latest and greatest ideas, so going over what's hot right now would be fruitless.

However, one of the largest trends today is eating healthy food. With the epidemic of obesity in America, it is important that you, the event planner, do not run the risk of contributing to this. One way to help is to find the American Heart Association guidelines for food and recipes, for example, and work with their list.

Healthy dining choices are also known to strengthen your productivity. Here are a few ideas you can put into practice without much thought:

- Serve low-calorie and low-fat foods
- Provide lean protein
- Use quality carbohydrates
- Have chef cook with healthy fats
- Serve more fruits and vegetables whenever possible
- Use low-fat cheeses
- Ask for soups and sauces to be made from a vegetable broth or low-fat milk rather than cream
- Server smaller portions
- Present vegetarian options
- Use an egg substitute or eliminate the yokes
- Use skim or 1 percent low-fat milk

The other part of healthy eating is eating local, sustainable and organic. Fresh, seasonal ingredients grown close to home are also very popular among the event-going public. Today, a typical meal travels 1,500 miles from farm to fork. Shrinking the distance to 100 miles is a lofty goal, but in some places, it can be done. Obviously, there are reasons why this cannot be done everywhere, including weather and actual location. But it may also be cost-prohibitive. Try your best, and work with your chef and within your budget.

There is also a small trend where hotels and restaurants are growing their own vegetables and herbs. They will be using other local ingredients such as eggs, honey, fresh fish, and free-range beef and chicken.

ENERGIZING AND GOOD MOOD FOODS

To help your participants maintain energy and focus during long days of meetings, it is important to serve quality food throughout the day. This helps them to retain what they are hearing and to be more of a participant and interact with others. When you are providing the food, serving your participants every three to four hours is optimal. Try to avoid processed or sugary carbohydrates (muffins, pastries, cookies, etc.). Instead, for breaks, serve fruits, nuts and cheeses. They won't give you that quick rush of energy that is always followed by the quick crash.

Some foods to fit into your meals when possible:
→ Salmon
→ Tofu
→ Yogurt (check the ingredients)
→ Chicken
→ Spinach
→ Coffee
→ Avocado
→ Berries (blueberries, strawberries, raspberries, and this years' queen of berries, acai berry)

Talk with the chef about other mood-enhancing and memory-improving foods. Also try to have water available everywhere. Dehydration lowers your energy.

Guaranteeing your numbers

As your event nears, you will be required to give the venue your estimated number of participants. You will pay for the number of meals that you set, even if there are no-shows. The final numbers are usually required 72 hours before the event. Typically, a facility will prepare for 3 to 10 percent above the number you submit depending on the size of your group. The larger the group, the fewer extra meals they will prepare.

The amount of food and money that is wasted during an event can be excessive. While donating leftover food to charitable organizations makes us feel good, ordering appropriately from the beginning and making the effort to guarantee accurately is a skill that can reduce costs significantly and is environmentally fitting.

Factors that can impact your numbers

What to watch for that will impact the number of people attending meal functions, especially for a multi-day event:

- Watch the number of hotel departures for each day of the meeting. Those departing that day will most likely not be attending that night's dinner function.

- Pay attention to the weather forecast. A beautiful day will encourage attendees to skip a banquet lunch function, while a rainy or cold day will cause most to attend.

- Know what is around the venue and the city. People like to sight-see when they are away and the more interesting things there are to do, the more people will adventure out of meetings and meal functions.

- Pay attention to the timing of the function. If sessions end at 5 p.m. and a reception starts at 7 p.m., many attendees will not come back.

- Programming also affects guarantee management. Featuring a speaker, entertainment or awards presentation during a meal function will encourage more attendees to participate.

Working with the Venue and Caterer

Although the catering manager, convention services manager, food and beverage director, chef, food vendors, and hired caterer will have wonderful suggestions, keep the following tips in mind to get the best value and make sure meals, banquets, coffee breaks, and receptions are to your satisfaction.

- Consult with the chef for ideas and special requests. Create your own list of options. You do not have to order off the menu.

- Choose healthy and high-quality foods that are in season.

- For large, important meal functions, make arrangements to do a tasting. Most facilities will allow advance taste testing. Do a tasting, especially if you are indecisive about a couple of selections.

- Know the food and beverage policies. Find out what is allowed. Most facilities will charge a fee to bring your own food and beverage, or they will simply not allow you to do so. Some organizations print their logo on prepackaged food and beverages and distribute these items to the participants. Try to negotiate this, if possible. It can amount to considerable savings.

- Find out how many servers and bartenders will be assigned to your functions. Service levels vary from facility to facility.

- Consider the appropriate type of service for a meal. Need a quick lunch? A box lunch might be the answer. Want people to mingle? Try a buffet. Service can vary according to an event's aims and goals. When buffets are used, make sure that the line is double and that there is at least one double-sided buffet line for every 75 to 100 people.

- Use decorative props and themes for breaks and meals. Ask the event venue about decorations in its inventory. Try to negotiate free use of these materials or rent props from event-planning companies.

- All meeting facilities have banquet menus. You will have the option of selecting plated meals, buffets, break packages, and à la carte items. They are sold either at a per-person price or by the dozen, gallon or piece. All prices are then subject to applicable service charge or gratuity and taxes. Find out the tax and service charge or gratuity percentages, and factor them into your budget. On average, they are 20 to 30 percent of the total food and beverage bill.

- Get menus in the beginning of the booking process, and review prices and options. Ask about the catering policies and a general information sheet. These explain specific food and beverage policies and might include their deadlines for receiving your menu selections, guarantees of attendance, table linen choices, floral arrangements, ice carvings, coat checks, extra labor charges, liquor liability issues, and liability statements.

- Negotiate firm menu prices when you book an event at a facility. Most facilities will guarantee food and beverage prices six to nine months in advance. You can request a guarantee for current menu prices or get a date through which prices are guaranteed.

Cost-Cutting Suggestions

With food and beverage playing such an important role in most events, this section will assist you in cutting your costs while maintaining quality and satisfaction. We have to remember our purpose and preserve our goals and objectives. Perhaps money is not an object for your event, but it is likely that these suggestions can reduce waste, suggest ideas for more appropriate choices, and provide tips for working with the professionals.

General suggestions

When looking to lower the price of your lunch or dinner, request a six-ounce instead of eight-ounce chicken breast or steak. Reducing the portion size of the accompanying side dishes does not help at all. Have heaping sides of rice, pasta, potatoes or other delicious non-meat plates. Instead of serving dessert at lunch, serve cookies, brownies or something sweet at the afternoon break.

When there is another larger group in the same hotel, it is often common that the smaller group can be served the same menu as the larger group. This is called "ganging," and it is possible the facility may reduce the price of your meal if you choose this option.

Buffet meals are more expensive than plated meals. You can also choose a less expensive meal but make it more formal by requesting a formal service style. While there may be service charges associated with more formal service, the savings on the menu price may more than make up for them.

Strategically located tables can alter the amount of food consumed, whether it is a breakfast buffet, refreshment breaks, or reception stations. Place them where they are not so readily accessible for seconds or thirds. Placing more expensive items in harder to access places can reduce consumption, such as placing shrimp or carving stations at the back of the room for receptions.

There is a very fine line you can cross here when trying to save costs. If food and beverage are too difficult to access, especially if there are long lines, you are likely to receive negative feedback and complaints from your participants.

Order bulk portions versus per person items, especially for continental breakfasts and refreshment breaks. While it is easier for planners to order based on the number of people attending, per person packages are more expensive because facilities must provide enough food for the number of people you have guaranteed regardless of whether the food is consumed.

Receptions and cocktail parties

Cocktail receptions with hors d'oeuvres and liquor can be one of the most difficult food and beverage functions to manage in terms of cutting costs without reducing quality. However, a few tips can help:

- Use butler-style service for hors d'oeuvres.
- Use smaller plates on buffet tables — less will be consumed.
- Put more expensive items toward the back of the room.
- Use cheese platters and crudités. They offer a large amount of food for less price.
- Use tray service for wine and soft drinks near the entrance, with full-service bars in the back. People who start with wine out of convenience will continue.

- Shorten cocktail parties and receptions — even 15 minutes can save you money.
- Use drink tickets instead of an open bar. Give each participant two or three tickets.
- Beer and wine are less expensive than hard liquor.
- Instruct bartenders not to serve doubles.
- When it comes to hors d'oeuvres, try fewer choices in larger quantities rather than a large selection in smaller quantities. Remember to avoid shrimp. People inhale it.
- Avoid salty foods during receptions as it encourages people to drink more.
- Go for domestic rather than imported wines and beer. Use house brands rather than premium.
- Check whether the hotel has deadstock wine available (wine that is no longer on the wine list). You may be able to negotiate a great price for some high-quality wine.

Serving wine

Wasting wine is very typical when precautions are not taken. With controlled conditions, having wine with dinner can be possible without breaking the bank. Take these tips into consideration:

- Open one bottle of each type of wine at a time.
- Start wine service after the salad or appetizer is served.
- Offer the wine. Do not just pour for everyone.
- Only refill wine when asked.
- Consider limiting the total number of bottles. Instruct servers to consult the planner when more is asked for.

- Have time limit for service. Suspend the wine service at a specific time, especially if it is late in the dinner.

Coffee breaks and continental breakfasts

There are many ways to reduce spending for these meal functions. Be creative and work with the venue to assist with these recommendations: Order "on consumption" when possible for bottled water, soda, and prepackaged food items such as granola bars, bags of chips, yogurt, whole fruit, power bars, cookies, and brownies. Or eliminate the bottled water, and serve water in a pitcher.

In some facilities, one gallon of coffee can cost $90 to $120, and the same price may be charged for hot water. Purpose and advanced planning are needed to result in significant savings. Order only what is needed, based on the number of people, the time of day, and the demographics of the group, and put controls in place for replenishing these beverages.

A gallon of coffee, decaf or hot water provides 18 to 20 cups. Depending upon the length of the event, you can figure two cups per person of coffee/decaf/tea combined. Again, knowing your audience is the key to your ordering suitable amounts.

Younger groups tend to consume more soft drinks than coffee, which means coffee orders can be reduced. Many facilities either automatically replenish coffee as it is consumed or replenish at specific times to original levels. Specify exact procedures for refilling beverages, such as checking with you before replenishing, not replenishing anything in the last five to ten minutes of a continental breakfast or refreshment break, or replenishing a certain amount of coffee/decaf/hot water at a certain time.

When food is left over from the continental breakfast, have it stored and used at the mid-morning breaks and likewise for leftovers from the morning break saved and used for the afternoon break. Order items that can be purchased on a consumption basis only, or order them by the dozen for afternoon breaks.

A few more cost-saving tips:

- Use any leftover food, not purchased on consumption, for the next break. Items like breakfast breads can be reused and put out at the mid-morning break. Unused food can also be delivered to the staff office or donated to a local shelter or soup kitchen.
- Serve mini-Danishes, muffins and doughnuts, or cut larger servings in half. Many people (especially women and dieters) only want half to start with. Alternatively, serve a continental breakfast instead of a full breakfast buffet.
- Add yogurt or cereals to dress up a continental breakfast.
- Use packaged items at breaks and be charged for consumption only. They can be used again.
- Go for sodas rather than more expensive mineral waters.

Suggested timelines

The following are some time frames to take into consideration when creating your agenda for meal service. Generally speaking, follow these guidelines and as always, they vary depending on your group, your finances, your venue, and your original purpose. Use this as a starting point. Always defer to venue/ caterer for suggestions.

Type of function	Time allotment	Staff per person	Notes
Continental breakfast	30 minutes to 1 hour	One buffet and one server up to 120 people	
Full Breakfast	One hour if buffet,	1 server Sit down – 1 server per 30+ guests	Only about 50 percent of participants will attend. Buffet is best.
Breaks between meetings	Minimum of 30 minutes	One server up to 100 people	Time for restroom, phone calls, snacks, networking.
Lunch	Minimum of 90 minutes	Sit down – 1 server per 30+ guests	Partial preset tables are helpful.
Receptions	Variable depending on whether dinner is to follow.	One server per 50 people	Will depend how much food is served (or at all) and type of bar setup.
Dinner	Two hours	Sit down – 1 server per 30+ guests	If formal, increase staff – 1 per 20

Alcohol Liability

Every planner must consider the gravity of dealing with intoxicated participants, underage drinking, and drunk driving when providing alcohol at events. Whether inside a contained facility or outdoors and open to the public, beware of your risks. This is serious business, as you could be held responsible or sued if something were to go wrong. Most liquor laws mandate that it is an offense to allow individuals to become intoxicated or to serve individuals who are already intoxicated.

When you hire a venue or caterer to sell or serve alcohol at your event, be sure that the vendor is compliant with state and local licensing and insurance regulations. If your server organization has no insurance, you or your company may be responsible for monetary damages.

Perhaps the best way to reduce your liability is to create an environment that discourages overconsumption. For example, limit the number of bartenders, making it harder to get a drink. Hold functions earlier in the evening — perhaps from 5 to 6 p.m. — when people are less inclined to drink heavily, or limit receptions to one hour.

Here are some concerns, issues and suggestions you should be aware of when serving alcohol at your event.

- Do not purchase and serve alcohol yourself. Let the facility or caterer provide and serve the alcohol. Doing so yourself may be a less expensive route, but it increases your liability.

- Ask what the venue policies are for service and how servers have been trained.

- Follow certain steps to prevent overindulgence by placing tent cards at the bar urging attendees to exercise good judgment and drink responsibly.

- Provide transportation or designated drivers – even designated walkers, especially for those staying in the hotel but having trouble getting to their rooms without injuring themselves or abusing others verbally or physically.

- If off-site, or as participants leave event, include a safe transportation plan. Encourage designated driver programs.

- Liquor liability insurance is not covered by standard provisions of general liability insurance. A rider may be necessary for your event. Note: Coverage does not include situations in which alcohol service is in violation of a statute, ordinance or regulation; a minor is served; or an already intoxicated person is served.

- Put an indemnification clause in your contract with the facility or caterer providing and serving the alcohol, making it clear that the facility or caterer will indemnify, defend, and hold harmless the company from and against all liability arising from alcohol-related incidents.

- Bartenders and servers are not to serve any individuals who appear inebriated or under the influence of alcohol. Require servers to refuse service to intoxicated guests.

- If the event is outside, use only plastic glasses and aluminum cans to prevent glass from being used as weapons during fights.

- Permit only regular drinks – no doubles.

- Have a good selection of non-alcoholic and low-alcohol beverages available at a reduced rate or complimentary.

- Price non-alcoholic drinks at a 40 percent discount from drinks containing alcohol.

- Eliminate last call to avoid guests from stocking up before the bar closes.

Outdoor events serving or selling alcohol present different challenges, especially when the event is open to the public and in an area with no specific perimeters or fencing to contain the crowd. Balancing fun and festivities with responsible planning is imperative.

Secure your site. Alcohol-related risks can present themselves even before the participant enters the event. Hire uniformed security staff to monitor outside areas such as parking lots to prevent intoxicated participants from entering the venue or driving away.

Good monitoring of IDs is also a must. It is helpful to have clear, concise rules posted at the entrance regarding general conduct and alcohol in particular. Train your staff on the procedures and guidelines that you established for your event.

Many groups and organizers learn the hard way about alcohol problems and liability. When your event suffers from fights, injuries or citations related to drinking, the quality of your event is jeopardized. Plan ahead, and be prepared with guidelines, insurance and security. Take all the precautions possible.

Marketing, Networking and Technology

Marketing and Networking

Getting the word out and carrying your message to potential guests is essential! Whether your participants are invited, required to attend, or willing to pay to come to your event, they need to know what your event is all about. They need to know when, where, why, how much, and what they should wear. Good marketing and promotion will be your vehicle to carry your message. This allows prospective participants to understand what you are offering, why they need to attend, and what is in it for them. Are you offering something significant and meaningful? You must demonstrate the benefits and value of coming to your event throughout your marketing campaign. Make the information clear and understandable.

The defined purpose plays an important role in your message and all of your promotional material from this point. Your goals and objectives are repackaged into a positive marketing campaign. The message you are sending must be powerful, set the tone, embrace your potential participants and entice them to come.

From your planning sessions, you came up with some methods for "getting your message out." You may have decided it would be through advertisements, publicity, public relations, direct mail, an email blast, or social networking. Use what works best for you and your event.

Knowing and reaching your target market is important, but successfully getting the message to them clearly is always a challenge. Depending on the type of event, you will have all sorts of participants: Some will be required to come, some will pay their own way, some will come at the expense of their companies, and some will just be invited free of charge. Regardless of their reason for coming, you must reach them with an effective and timely invitation.

Your invitation should create anticipation and enthusiasm. It is the primary function of your message that will be reflected in every piece of material you produce. Your marketing and promotional material can come in hundreds of different styles and be delivered in as many ways. Most often it will include a registration form or a way to purchase tickets.

For many events, marketing is handled by an individual or group of specialists. A non-profit organization may have a public relations committee, while a corporation might have a marketing department or director on staff. Larger corporations may have a public relations firm or advertising company on retainer. Whether you are doing it yourself or working with others, make a plan. Start early when designing your promotional material. Do not miss important deadlines because your marketing copy is not ready.

Promoting Your Event

Marketing and publicity material is imperative to promotion of your event. The material you create essentially invites someone to come to your event by providing as much information as possible about what it offers and how to become a participant. Your invitation can be a poster, a blog, an announcement through social media, a party invitation, a full-color brochure, a one-page flyer, a radio spot, a newspaper ad, or all the above. The choice is yours. Just get the message out.

Simple or complicated, there are hundreds of ways to get your message out. The key is to give you enough time to create the material successfully and completely. There is nothing worse than sending out 5,000 flyers only to discover you put the wrong phone number in the text.

Weigh the benefits of advertising dollars versus memorable amenities. Consider carefully, do you really need that four-page full color brochure that will cost an arm and a leg, or would you rather create a smaller, less expensive piece and spend the savings on something special for the participants? Will social networking and a high-class Web page be sufficient? Making the event more exciting and memorable might be worth more than the marketing material. They will not remember the brochure as much as the trio singing in the background during lunch or the delicious croissants served every morning with freshly brewed rich coffee.

When I was doing sporting events, I found that one of the best ways to get to my target market was to attend similar events and go around the parking lot and place flyers under the windshield wipers of each car. Each flyer would have a registration form as well as all the information a participant would need to know about the event (time, place, event, cost, address, and phone number). I would mark each form with a code to let me know where it came from. This way I could keep track of where my efforts worked the best. This was well before the invention of websites or the Internet. But this type of marketing effort is still good today. Remember, use recycled paper, and note your website address. The key is to make it easy for people to participate.

Kathy T.
Naples, Florida

The marketing format used for the above sporting event also works well for music events, festivals, art shows and other outside events. If the telephone is not ringing, the online registration isn't getting sales, and the returned RSVP forms are not in your mailbox, you may need to do something different.

The flyer itself may be perfect, but it must be in the hands of the right people. The flyer may be reaching the right people but not doing a good enough job of motivating them to take action. The problem with this method of marketing is that it is hard to get feedback on what specifically you need to change.

Ask yourself, have you got the right brochure reaching the wrong people, the wrong brochure reaching the right people, or worst of all, the wrong brochure reaching the wrong people! One thing for sure is that when you have the right brochure reaching the right people, you are well on your way to ensuring that your next event is a raging success.

Publicity and word of mouth are the least risky and most effective means of promotion, and this is where social media and networking can play a large role. Send press releases to the media or to your potential participants about your event. Be specific, and grab their attention. Send this information to other business and organizations as well, and let them network for you.

This guide is not going to tell you that you need advertising or the type of advertising you need, but we have listed different styles of advertising options. You will know whether you need advertising from your defined purpose and the type of event you are having. But most importantly, will advertising be worth the money? While advertising is the most expensive form of getting the word out, used wisely and appropriately, it can be extremely effective.

Keep in mind the power of the Internet. Creating a website, blog, Facebook page or Twitter account can be forms of publicity and networking. You can reach an unlimited number of people. Your potential participants can access your information 24/7, and it can also be used as a multi-layered resource for conference registration, accommodations and air travel.

When it comes to your website, people expect the ability to go there and find all the information they need to participate. Make it easy to use, informative and attractive with your message stated loudly and clearly. Use your website address in all of your promotional material.

TIPS ON PUBLICITY

The Do's and Don'ts of Media Follow-Up - 15 Things the Media Loves / Hates

The way you handle the media is the key to achieving desired success. They are finicky. Aim for the headlines. What makes the media smile and what makes them cringe?

15 Things the media dislikes:
1) When pitching an event, not taking "no" for an answer
2) Long news releases
3) Lying, hype, and misrepresentations of your event
4) Lack of Preparation
5) Small Talk about your event
6) Overkill - don't send them every detail
7) No repeated cold calling
8) Freebies – don't overdo it with gifts
9) Name dropping
10) Lack of focus
11) Confirmation calls
12) Gimmicks
13) Not following up requests
14) Same ideas
15) Getting upset that they say no

15 Things the media loves:
1) News – be specific why your event fits the news
2) Brevity and clarity – give them the specifics about the event
3) Knowing targets
4) Relationships
5) Preparation
6) Broad appeal
7) Ties – how does your event tie into the news
8) Experience
9) Visualization
10) Celebrity tie-ins

11) Prompt response
12) Courtesy
13) Visual aids
14) No road blocks
15) A pleasant attitude

Jill Lublin is an international speaker on the topics of Radical Influence, Publicity, Networking and referrals

MORE TIPS ON PUBLICITY

Getting the word out will be one of your top priorities. The person in charge of publicity has to be tenacious, charming, blessed with writing skills, and most importantly, organized.

Magazines: Is there a magazine whose readers might attend your event? Contact them ASAP. Travel magazines and those published by auto clubs are excellent targets. Since most have at least a three-month lead time, start early!

Events Column: If the newspaper has one, send them the basics: what is the event, the date(s), the time; mention a few highlights to grab interest; admission charge (if it is free, say so!); location and brief directions (for example, the Podunk Fairgrounds: take the Podunk exit off Route 66, and follow the signs). If possible, include a website or email for people to make contact for more information.

Features: If you have good pictures of a segment of your event and can write an accompanying story, send the Features Editor a query. Briefly explain your event, stating why you believe the magazine's readers would enjoy it, and offer to submit the story — again, months in advance! They may take you up on it!

Newspapers: Start contacting every newspaper within a 200-mile radius. (If your event is that special, yes they will come!) Learn the name, email and phone number of entertainment editors about six months in advance, and keep in touch with them about every two or three weeks. Congratulate them on a feature that is related to your event, and request guidelines for submitting press releases. It is important to keep the lines of communication open because newspaper people can come and go. This way, if the original editor leaves, you will find out the name of the new one right away and still have a viable resource.

This is where writing skills are needed. Editors are very busy people. Their reporters are frantically finishing last-minute articles on late breaking news. Should you send them a well-written piece before their deadline, it is one less article they have to come up with and stands a very good chance of getting published.

TV: Even if your event is for only one day, after people see it on the 6 o'clock news, they will make note of it for next year! Get in touch with your local TV stations. This takes a real people-person, because you have to be persistent and upbeat all the time. Who is the man or woman who always shows up at events, telling viewers what a fun activity it is? That is the person you get in touch with. Try emailing or phoning them, and keep it up until you make contact. Tell them how much you enjoy their coverage of events! Then mention yours, and give a few camera-worthy highlights. If your event has an admission fee, tell them they will of course get in free with their camera crew. Ask if they have some free time in the morning or afternoon and offer to come to the station to bring them some more information on the event — brochures and posters. If that is not possible, mail them a nice packet of data. If your event involves T-shirts, find out what size they wear, and bring or send them one!

Here is a good strategy: Should one of the local stations agree to cover your event, casually mention this to other stations as well, since you do not want them to miss out. No network affiliate likes to be scooped by a rival. If one shows up, the other just may come too. Make sure that all news crews are provided passes, and assign someone with your event to be each one's guide. Suggest alternate points of interest so that they film different portions of the event.

The Invitation

Your invitation and marketing media can include the registration form, ads, social networking sites, publicity, brochures, blogs, your website, emails, flyers, press releases, interoffice memos, posters, formal invitations, evites, or even a phone call. There are hundreds of styles, shapes, sizes, colors, and sounds that can be used to get your message out. This is the time to get creative. Keep in mind your goals and objectives.

If your event is simple, you many need just the date, time, place, and objective. "Come to the crab feed on Friday the 13th at the boat club at 5 p.m. BYOB! RSVP required – call 555-1212."

But it can also be very complicated. You may need to create the brochure to convey the information about your event. If it is a professional event, make the brochure professional. If your event is whimsical and entertaining, make the material the same. If you work with a designer, be sure to communicate your intent and share the purpose. With the ease of desktop publishing today, many people can design these materials themselves. Be sure to include all the pertinent information in your promotional material no matter what type of invitation. Can you imagine sending out 1,500 mailers without a time or location for the event? Even a misspelled name can be embarrassing. It could be a disastrous mistake. Read and re-read your material before it is printed.

To capture the reader's attention and solicit interest, use the following tips when creating your material. These remain the same regardless of the marketing form you are using.

- **Attention**: Attract the reader's attention! Use color, dramatic photos, over- or under-sized material, clever words, unusual paper, or interesting fonts.

- **Interest**: Offer a solution! The reader's interest is directly linked to a need or a desire. Offer the solution with a clearly stated understanding of their reward, such as education, a fun time, and/or a chance to meet like-minded people.

- **Desire**: State the benefits clearly. What's in it for them? The more benefits, the better.

- **Action**: Clear directions will make the reader take action. They may be in the form of commands such as, "Save the date!" or "Call and register now!" or "Mark your calendars now!"

- **Copy**: This is your sales pitch with benefits clearly outlined. Find a strong meeting title and descriptive subtitles. Provide pertinent meeting data: goals, objectives, registration information, the date, and times.

Use creative graphics. Whether it is a "save the date" postcard, direct mail brochure, Facebook invitation or an evite blast, use colorful graphics to grab the attention of your attendees. For postcards, put slogans and graphics on both sides because there is a 50/50 chance the postcard will land face down on a desk.

Event: Fundraiser

Location: Several years ago, I was arranging for a 151-foot sailboat to dock at several ports around the San Francisco Bay. At each port, the public would board the ship and sail with the crew around the Bay. Each trip was to raise awareness and money to support a journey from Hawaii to Pennsylvania via the Panama Canal. The ship was filled with young underprivileged boys on a purpose quest. At the last minute, before the scheduled times were about to be printed in the marketing material, we realized that the ship's hull was too deep for a couple of the piers. Fortunately, we were able to reserve other piers with deeper water and change the times slightly to adjust for the tides. We had forgotten to check the tide chart!

Luckily, we were able to change the times and locations before the printed materials and press releases were sent out. It kept us from having to reprint brochures and saved us quite a bit of money.

Anonymous

Put your registration in the invitation

Decide early on whether you want online or paper registration. It almost sounds archaic to have paper registration, but some people still do it because it serves a purpose. Not everyone is technically savvy or even has a computer. If you have the capability to do the online registration, do it. It will save you a great deal of time and money. See the *References* section, under Management Resources, for suggestions of online registration software and companies who offer that service. Or have a web designer create a unique form just for your event.

However, having paper registration is still essential. With respect to collecting fees, get a system set up right at the start. Make sure the information in the registration form is clear and simple to interpret. Having to reimburse or collect more money is time-consuming. Will you need to set up a PayPal account or take credit cards or personal checks?

Address the following in the registration form:

- Is payment required at the time of registration?
- Tell them how to make out the check.
- Do you accept credit cards? If so, be sure to have a place for the number and expiration date and a signature.
- Checks must be in U.S. dollars only.
- Cancellation policy. Under what conditions and at what date are there no refunds?
- Identify all costs above registration fee. For example, extra meals, excursions or upgrades.
- Spell-out what the registration fee covers: breaks, reception, registration materials, meals, parking, airport transfers.
- Include specific instructions on how to register and when, and price savings if registering early.
- Tell them how they will receive their confirmation.

A couple of ways to attract more attendees is by announcing this information in your marketing and registration information. Using price reductions for multiple participants can bring your numbers up. To make it easier for organizations to send multiple attendees, give a discount for multiple registrations. Think of sliding discounts for every additional person after the first registrant. The first person pays full price, but if they send two, three or more, the reduction kicks in.

Extend your early-bird rate. Build in some wiggle room for an early-bird rate, and as the date approaches, extend it by a few weeks. People are inclined to leap when they think they are getting a second chance.

Designing Your Website

If you do not already have a website, build one now, or hire someone to do it for you! They are cheaper and easier than ever before. Companies that offer template pages can walk you through the process for the price of monthly hosting fees. It is fairly easy these days.

The easiest and fastest way a participant can register or buy tickets for your event is through your website. This means not only having a website but having one that is easy to navigate and filled with all the information a participant may want. The site must provide all necessary data because you want them to register then and there.

Usability and effective communication are the most important factors in the success of your Web page. This includes making content easy to find and giving users everything they need to know. The easier it is for participants to find what they are looking for, the more people you will attract. Too often, websites focus on looking attractive or quirky instead of understanding the true needs of customers. People are so busy today that they truly want straightforwardness and simplicity.

Here is a list of four small event and business web design trends:

1. **Minimalist** design effectively strips away the excess and helps the user concentrate squarely on the content. If a page has too many elements,

the user will easily become confused about where to focus, with many elements vying for attention.

2. Use custom **photography** or artwork whenever possible. For small events and businesses, both time and budget are limited, and stock photos are a relatively cheap — or even free — and accessible resource.

3. Web design at its core is about communication, and **typography** is a vital component of that. Great Web typography helps bring order to information and creates a coherent, visually satisfying experience that engages the reader without their knowing.

4. You want to grab your visitor's attention and move him or her to take action. Crafting a clear, concise **call to action** is essential.

Online registration

Registration used to require hours of database management, postage, sorting, and paperwork. Today, online registration has revolutionized the process and in doing so, increased customer service. Customers have 24/7 access to your website, can register, and get immediate confirmation. Once they are in the database, your keeping in contact with them is trouble-free, creating their name tag is a breeze, and creating the participant roster is simplified.

MONEY SAVING TIPS

➥ Use online registration.

➥ Design brochures and programs in-house. Give the printer a flash drive or CD to eliminate proofreading and typesetting errors.

➥ Keep design and format to regular-sized paper. Odd-size brochures cost more to produce.

➥ Use bulk mail for large mailing. Make sure you have plenty of time for mail to arrive.

➥ Use technology when appropriate for marketing, registration and normal communication.

➥ Check with the Convention and Visitor Bureaus for photos or artwork. They often lend them out at no charge.

Reaching Your Target Market

Whether your potential participants are individuals or groups of people, it is better to invite more people than to limit your marketing efforts. Use your marketing dollars wisely so that you can maximize profitability while effectively enticing prospects to attend. Consider:

- Who is your target audience?
- What business are they in?
- Which groups of people would be willing to pay to hear this information?
- Where are they?
- How do I find them?
- What is the best method to reach them?

Your intended participants should have the ability to pay and the desire to attend your event. Do not waste money on those outside your target market.

There are hundreds of leads in any given marketplace. The trick is to go find them. After you have determined your target market, begin compiling a networking campaign to go after them. The beginning of this process will be time-consuming but well worth your efforts.

One way to gather leads is through your own personal set of connections. Search organizations and business associations you belong to, business clubs, your friends and family members, or your Rolodex (yes, they still exist). You can also buy lists of particular segments of the population or use lists from past events. With the ease of online registration, maintaining and reusing lists is easy.

Promoting a Global Event

Marketing an event overseas can be demanding and challenging. Making your content and topics attractive to an international audience will be different from marketing stateside. International events can be one of the most rewarding aspects of your career and will open up a world of experiences. Embrace the culture of the country where you are holding your event from the beginning.

What works in the United States will not necessarily work overseas. Plan your event with global awareness from the start. Integrate an on-site local advisory board and local facility into your program and use local key opinion leaders. They can be pivotal to raising awareness of your event and drawing participation. This is also a time to think about using a local destination management company for cultural guidance and direction.

Be very aware of the language you use when speaking and writing to your foreign co-workers, vendors, service providers and participants. We Americans have thousands of creative catchy phrases, alliterations, puns, plays on words and metaphors that may not connect with a foreign audience or translate clearly.

Pay attention to your images, hand gestures and symbols. Their meanings can vary widely from one culture to another. We might take them for granted to mean one thing, but they may be highly offensive to someone from another country. It might be a good idea to ask for assistance from local members before putting anything in print.

Marketing tactics that work for one particular country may not for another. Every culture connects with key messages in a different way. Take the time to discover how your potential participants learn about events before you invest in your marketing tactics. For instance, mail service in Mexico City is not reliable. Therefore, you want to market your event through the Internet rather than through a direct mail campaign. (Direct mail is not even used in Mexico as a marketing tactic.) Be polite, and mind your manners. The social aspect of events can be much more culturally important outside of the United States. You may find it challenging to stay within guidelines for meal expenditures. Also, pay careful attention to meal times. In Europe, if you plan a working lunch or allocate less than an hour for meals, you will be viewed as tactless. In Mexico, remember that people eat lunch around 4 p.m. If you try to schedule lunch at noon, people might perceive it as just a coffee break.

Each country has its unique culture, and the more homework you do to be aware of these distinctions, the better marketing material you will create, the more effective your promotion efforts will be, and the more appropriate the information you will share.

Visas requirements in flux

Keep attendees informed as much as possible of new rules and regulations and proper documentation they will need to follow for the event. Encourage them to continue to check the rules and laws before leaving the country because laws are subject to change. Perhaps give the participants the hosting country's embassy details for consultation. Because each country may have different admission requirements for nationals of different nations, it is very difficult for a sponsor to provide accurate information for every prospective attendee.

Timing

Timing is everything – START EARLY! Start early, and lay your groundwork. Do the marketing and networking that makes sense for your event. Some large organizations begin marketing years in advance. Some smaller events only need a few weeks or months, but try to get on people's calendars early. Being late with your promotions means poor attendance, a cancelled event or worst of all, a great deal of money lost.

Technology Speaking

The World of Technology

Event planners constantly use technology in every area of their business. It is critical to stay on top of the latest and greatest changes and improvements, new devices and gadgets, software and hardware, applications, social media and networking, and cloud storage and computing. When used properly, technology can enhance communication, bring people together more effectively, dazzle the audience, improve the learning environment, and broaden the scope of meetings and special events. Technology has made the process of bringing people together much easier and delivering the message more powerful. The trick is to know what to use and how and when to use it.

Event planning is no longer a business for the technically challenged. Just keeping up with the terminology is tricky and time-consuming. With the ever-increasing multi-functionality of gadgets and our hyper-connected culture, we need to be knowledgeable users. Do you carry a smartphone and a tablet? Do you still carry USB drives, or are you using cloud services? Just how techie are you?

Technology is evolving at supersonic speeds, enhancing the event and meeting industry and increasing the adaptability of event communications. A few of the newer tools are presentation management, webcasting, audience response system, video conferencing and radio-frequency identification (RFID). Using any of these tools in addition to your standard audiovisual equipment can boost your participants' ability to communicate effectively and maximize the success of your event.

How is your knowledge on social networking and social media? Are you using webcasting, live video streaming, holding virtual or hybrid meetings, blogging, producing webinars, or podcasting? Do you or your company have accounts on Facebook, Twitter, LinkedIn or Instagram? Or do you just get by with your simple email functions and word processing application and marketing through your website or a brochure? It is a whole new world out there — get on board. See the Section on Social Media and Networking.

The following chapter will bring you up-to-date on some of today's most popular technological advancements in the audiovisual world that can enhance your event planning. Improvements are being developed so quickly that by the time you have read this section, something bigger, better and faster will have hit the market. Either keep up, or bring in a savvy tech person or social media guru to help guide you. We will be speaking in general terms. This is not particularly a how-to chapter. This is an overview of what is out there and how it may augment what you are doing today.

Staying on Top of Technology

The way you plan, market, produce and measure your events is changing and always will. **We are experiencing the biggest shift in events, meetings and learning in decades!** A whole group of digital essentials are changing the way we do business.

Over the last five years, technology has changed so dramatically that sometimes it is hard to keep up. Technology has undoubtedly made our lives somewhat easier, but it has also created added work for planners. We need to stay on top of new and improved methods of communication so we can offer it to our participants.

Know What You Need

The first key to technology is being aware of what is available and knowing what you need for your particular event, be it audiovisual equipment, lighting, staging or Internet connection. When technology plays a large role in your event, do a survey of the venue before signing any contracts.

Meet with the network engineer or technical director as well as the venue's telecom manager for a tour. During the walkthrough, examine telecom closets, and record the locations of jacks, wireless access points and power drops. Itemize the cost of networking equipment such as routers, switches and networked computers. Then, examine the entire high-speed Internet access connectivity agreement carefully and put prices, service, deliverables and timetables in your contract. Find out what equipment and services that venue can offer you so you know whether you will need to hire an outside audiovisual company.

Audiovisual Services and Equipment

Let's look at audiovisual equipment and services first. Fast-forward from yesterday's standard audiovisual equipment such as microphones, overhead projectors, LCD projectors and the like, and you will find a new breed of technology available for business, educational meetings, and social and special events. It is not only important to keep up with what is available but to understand how to use it to enhance your events. Today, events are about much more than lights, camera, and action.

The design of your audiovisual and technology needs begins with concepts taken from the defined purpose of the event. From there, sketches and renderings, floor plans, and schematics are created, designating where everything

— stage lights, video, computer projection equipment, scenery and portable rest rooms — will be placed. The design will derive from client meetings as well as hotel or venue site evaluations, show and room limitations, electrical specifications, and your goals and objectives.

Your objective might be to promote your message clearly in a beautiful and artistic manner while impressing and winning over your audience. Or do you want to blast your audience out of their seats, wow them, and keep them talking long after the meeting has ended? Will you need fireworks? Laser lights? Theatrics? How about indoor, state-of-the-art, computer-controlled, intelligent lighting? Or do you just want the best lighting and sound for an outdoor birthday bash? Whatever you want, it is probably available, no matter how remote the location.

The mark of a professional event planner is that all aspects of your events run flawlessly, avoiding the most visible and annoying technology failure – and that means bringing in the best staff and professional technicians. They will install, maintain and operate all kinds of production equipment so that every detail is accounted for, right down to duct-taping the cable to the floor.

Whether the event is inside or outdoors, your technology needs can range from a single flipchart to a multi-media extravaganza using state-of- the-art equipment. When it is more than a flipchart, the event can require dozens of vendors involved in set-up, and installation can be expensive and time-consuming.

Terminology and definitions

Below are some terms that you will need to know when you order technical equipment and services for your event. Take the following request at a hotel for example:

"I will be requiring Internet capabilities via T1, DSL, or fiber optic circuit lines, all of which offer different bps rates, or do you have wireless." There are so many different options that you will need to know your special requirements.

Do you have any idea what that means? In reality, you may not need to know if you hire an audiovisual company or choose a venue with a savvy tech person on staff. But you will need to know what this is when it comes to working out the final bill. You need to know what you are paying for. Here is a look at some terms you might come across:

TECHNOLOGY TERMS	
Audience Response System	Offers interactive database programs that produce instant reports from live input. ARS enhances an event by involving the audience and offering a quick method to gather valuable information. For example, they can streamline complex voting procedures. Participants are given individual keypads and can answer multiple-choice questions or cast votes in real time, with results being tabulated and displayed moments later.
Bandwidth	The data transmission capacity of an electronic line. It is expressed in bits per second (bps).
Bps rate	Bits per second are a measure of the number of data bits (digital 0s and 1s) transmitted each second in a communications channel. This is usually in reference to modem speed.
Digital Lighting	Has specialized uses and can be very flexible.
DSL	DSL is short for digital subscriber line, which allows a modem to transform a plain telephone service line into a digital line and thus beef up bandwidth capability.
Fiber optic circuit	Data connectivity services for higher-bandwidth applications. It is a hair-thin glass strand designed for light transmission. It is capable of transmitting trillions of bits per second.

TECHNOLOGY TERMS	
HSIA	High-Speed Internet Access.
ISP	Internet Service Provider.
Kiosks	An interactive kiosk is an electronic communications tool that enables customers to serve themselves by accessing information, taking advantage of special offers, making purchases, or gathering information. Like an ATM.
LAN	Local Area Network
Portable Media Player	A PMP is a handheld audiovideo system that can record and playback from a TV, DVD player, camera or media file downloaded from the Internet, such as smartphones, tablets, MP3 players and other mobile devices.
RFID	Radio Frequency Identification Device uses access points to retrieve information remotely from special tags via radio waves. It captures data from up to 15 feet away. Used on name tags for tracking, control access, continuing education unit tracking, crowd flow tracking, traffic pattern reporting, and post-show demographic analysis.
RSS	RSS is defined as Really Simple Syndication or Rich Site Summary. RSS files are formed as XML files and are designed to provide content summaries of news, blogs, forums or website content.
Router	A router connects the T1 to an Internet Service Provider (ISP).
T1 lines	A high-speed Internet connection that is a dedicated copper circuit installed by the telephone company. Many hotels and other large venues are equipped with this service.
USB	Universal Serial Bus sends data to standard devices such as computers, but its popularity has prompted it to also become commonplace on video game consoles and smartphones as well as devices such as televisions, home stereo equipment (MP3 players), and portable memory devices.
USB Flash Drives	Data storage devices integrated with a USB interface. They are typically small, lightweight, removable and rewritable. USB flash drives have several advantages over other portable storage devices, particularly the floppy disk.
Wireless	Wireless Internet is a method of communication that uses low-powered radio waves to transmit data between devices. The term refers to communication without cables or cords, chiefly using radio frequency and infrared waves.

Presentation management

Presentation management is a service that directs the electronic presentation materials for educational sessions, training meetings, or any other event where multiple presenters are involved. Speakers submit their electronic presentations in advance via a secure website or on-site at the speaker-ready room. Presentations are electronically transmitted to the speakers' assigned session room, streamlining meetings by allowing planners to control the computer and audiovisual equipment used in meeting rooms. Presenters no longer need to bring their own computers, eliminating equipment compatibility issues, and once the presentations are collected in one central location, they can be easily assembled for webcasting, podcasting or educational purposes after the event.

Using kiosks

There is a growing public awareness of value-added services of kiosks that are everywhere today. You find them at airports, hotels and when you pick up your rental car. You see them at the bank, in the supermarket, and in your local mall. National parks, libraries, post offices and other government agencies use kiosks. They are becoming very common technology in our daily lives.

What are they, and how are they being used in the event planning arena? They can enhance your event by delivering a welcome message and information, providing local entertainment and sightseeing details, publishing promotions, providing travel information by supplying airline links, providing exhibitor and booth information, offering coupons, and displaying and updating agendas. They are being used at large convention centers, hotels, trade shows, conferences, sporting events, festivals, and concerts.

They are also being used to allow participants to make comments and submit evaluations. Can you think of other ways to use them?

Internet Access

Almost everyone in our society uses the Internet. For corporate and business events, having Internet access is a necessity. Nowadays, providing wireless service to the participants to use with their own laptops, smartphones and other tablet devices is expected and universal.

When you need Internet access, decide how you will provide the service, how much bandwidth is necessary, how and where the computers will be set up, and how many you need. If you will be webcasting, choose your venue based on your webcast needs. Not all hotels and venues are set up for your technology needs.

Where will the access points be placed — in the meeting rooms, around the community area of the venue, sleeping rooms, or all of the above? What kind of high-speed access is needed? Is high-speed Internet access required in the meeting rooms for presentations? You must determine whether the requirements are for the planners, the participants, the presenters, the entertainers, the vendors or all the above.

If a speaker needs to download presentations, slides or graphics, the venue's T1 or DSL lines must be sufficiently fast and secure. Planners are able to order more or less bandwidth depending on the complexity of the meeting.

Many international, national, and regional hotels, motels, and resort chains are adding free Wi-Fi and high-speed Internet access as an amenity for guests and meeting planners. In addition to wireless in guest rooms, they offer access in a variety of public locations, such as lobbies, meeting rooms, restaurants and lounges. Each site will vary. Find out where the access begins and ends. You may want your non-hotel guests to have access while they are attending your event as well.

Types of bandwidth

T1 is the standard on-site high-speed Internet access available at most venues today. A switch then enables the T1 to be fractionalized or shared between meeting rooms via the venue's wiring. Venues that are not currently wired for T1 are able to secure temporary lines for clients, though they are expensive and time-consuming to install.

Fiber offers the most capacity but is rare to find in most venues right now. Even though it is costly to install, it will become the standard for on-site HSIA in the near future. If you want the benefits of enormous capacity, lower cost, and a more secure service now, find a venue with fiber-optic circuit installed.

Inquire as to what is shared on the lines. If the hotel's sleeping rooms share bandwidth with your meeting rooms, you can have a significant deceleration right in the middle of an important presentation or when doing other vital work such as printing badges, handling registration or updating the latest spreadsheet. If the hotel does not budge on allocating a full T1 line to you, then consider hiring an outside information technology (IT) company or have the hotel create a DSL line to get a dedicated non-sharing circuit.

The cost of access

Know the going rates and what is negotiable for Internet connectivity. It is recommended that when deciding on effective technology, planners get technical advice from IT experts who specialize in digital events. It is crucial that every planner have a working knowledge of technology costs after decisions are made with the IT expert, the venue or the outside technical consultant.

Internet access can be an expensive portion of your event. If you know the approximate costs, you can negotiate with confidence with your venue and save money. To negotiate, be prepared with a lower amount competitive venues are charging or the fact that others offer more service for the same price. Of course, it is understood and respected that a venue needs to be compensated and make revenue, but there is a difference between that and price gouging a naive meeting planner.

Using Virtual Events

Podcasting, webcasting, teleseminars, webinars, video streaming and the technologies associated with them are custom-made for event professionals. We will group them together and refer to them as virtual events. They are a way to get your event out to others who are unable to attend your event or who want the information for later use. They can watch or listen live or at their leisure.

Digitally recorded virtual meetings are enhanced versions of the audio tape recording. Because they are high quality, they can be used by organizations and associations to distribute information to members who are unable to attend the meeting. Virtual meetings are easily downloaded from your website for free or for a fee.

When is a virtual event good for business? When you have a website, a digital recording, and an audience wanting your content, you have the key components to virtual event. Virtual events distribute content to people who want the information in a format they can easily use. As long as they have Internet access, the audience can be anywhere in the world. It even allows the participant to listen to the information at their leisure through their smartphone or tablets.

Virtual events can function as a revenue generator or a value-added feature for clients and attendees. In the days of analog recording, conference attendees would buy audio tapes of sessions. The sound quality was usually poor and the fast-forward and rewind features made it difficult to isolate the content that was really needed. All of that has changed with virtual events. The sound is impeccably clear and navigating through the material is simple.

A bonus is that you can include visuals such as slides or video from a session and additional content such as background information about the speaker that audio tape recordings just cannot provide. The digital format allows users to create their own experience with the media by picking and choosing what content they want to use. Users are younger and more tech-savvy than ever, and they have high standards when it comes to digital media.

Webcasting services provide a powerful and progressive addition to live events by expanding the audience and enhancing the program even for those in attendance. Events can be streamed live or archived for later viewing in audio only or audio/video formats. Registration options capture relevant information about viewers as well as prevent unauthorized access to content by requiring viewers to enter a password to view the event.

Video conferencing presents an opportunity to have meetings without having to travel. The benefits inspire people to communicate more effectively and efficiently and ultimately make organizations more productive. Besides saving time, it also decreases cost, reduces travel time, encourages collaboration and stimulates communication.

These types of meetings are great for short information exchange, however, with your multi-tasking audience, whose attention spans are short, you should be kept to no more than 45 minutes. Even a 30-minute event is about the maximum someone is willing to sit in front of their computer screen.

Descriptions of virtual events

VIRTUAL REALITY OF DISTRIBUTING AND RECEIVING INFORMATION	
Blog	A **blog** (a blend of the term *web log*) is a type of website or part of a website. Blogs are usually maintained by an individual with regular entries of commentary, descriptions of events or other material, such as graphics or video.
Hybrid Event	Where a live event is coinciding with a virtual event.
Podcasting	The distribution of audio or video files, such as radio programs, lectures and classes, or music videos over the Internet for listening on mobile devices and computers.
Social Networking Services	An online service, platform, or site that focuses on building and reflecting of social networks or social relations among people. For example, people who share interests and/or activities. A social network service essentially consists of a representation of each user (often a profile), his/her social links, and a variety of additional services. Most social network services are Web-based and provide means for users to interact over the internet, such as email and instant messaging.
Telepresence	A type of teleconferencing developed by Cisco Systems that goes beyond the traditional screen-to-screen experience. By using high-definition video and audio, it creates the illusion that participants are sitting in the same room.
Telepresence suites	Major hotel chains have begun offering business suites equipped with virtual equipment in heavy business markets.

VIRTUAL REALITY OF DISTRIBUTING AND RECEIVING INFORMATION	
Teleseminar	A teleseminar is a telephone conference call. Attendees call at a set time (not toll-free). The presenter calls in and begins their presentation. The advantage of attending a teleseminar is the ability to bring a group of people together from all over the nation from the comfort of your own home or office.
Video Conferencing	A **videoconference** or **video conference** (also known as a *videoteleconference*) is a set of interactive telecommunication technologies which allow two or more locations to interact via two-way video and audio transmissions simultaneously.
Virtual Meeting	Expand the reach and have access to information 24/7. **Web conferencing** is used to conduct live meetings, training or presentations via the Internet. In a web conference, each participant sits at his or her own computer and is connected to other participants via Internet. This can be either a down-loaded application on each of the attendees' computers or a web-based application where the attendees access the meeting by clicking on a link distributed by email (meeting invitation) to enter the conference.
Webcasting	The transmission of linear audio or video content over the Internet. A webcast uses streaming media technology to take a single content source and distribute it to many simultaneous listeners and viewers.
Webinars	Similar to webcasting or teleseminar. Used to capture a recording to use for client support archives or for use as a saleable product.

Hybrid Events

A hybrid event is a tradeshow, conference, un-conference, seminar, workshop or other meeting that combines a "live" in-person event with a "virtual" online component. Done right, it can be a great advantage for those who cannot travel but want to participate and want the content you are offering.

With the growing popularity and cost-effectiveness of virtual events, hybrid events have become a popular way of increasing participation in traditional events at a relatively low cost. They also enable participation by people who might be unable to attend physically due to travel or time zone constraints or desire to reduce the carbon footprint of the event. The open, participatory nature of un-conferences and their focus on sharing content makes them hybrid events, too.

Generally, the virtual component involves an online representation of the live event. For example, online participants might have access to:

- Live audio or video streaming of keynote speakers or workshops
- Online presentations
- Creation of a live commentary or transcript of proceedings
- Online chat or discussion forum facilities
- Live blogs
- Event photographs and video
- Integration of other social media tools such as Twitter, LinkedIn, Facebook, etc.

Provision of Internet access, usually via free Wi-Fi, is normal at hybrid events. As well as allowing a physical event to reach a wider audience, these online tools also provide a means for physical attendees to interact with each other, event organizers and online participants, as well as a way for online participants to interact with each other.

Event content can also be recorded and made available online to foster further discussions after the event has ended.

Technology Trends and a Look Ahead

Some things we can look forward to:

Mobile Apps – Almost everyone has at least one mobile device with them at all times. Being connected is a way of life today and more so in the future. At this time, there are few usable event apps and much room for improvement for existing apps. Currently, they are good at:

1. Replacing paper such as programs, agendas, list of attendees, exhibitor guides, handouts, course notes, taking surveys, evaluations, providing onsite maps, venue layouts and more.

2. Onsite networking, pre-event networking, alerts and announcements, per-to-peer messaging, contact exchange, and social media engagement.

Analyzing Data – With the above improvements to mobile app capabilities, instant data will be available. You will be able to see trending topics, favorite speakers, frequently used app features, and specific statistics on surveys and polls.

Bluetooth (BLE=Bluetooth low energy) – ibeacons and geofencing with traffic tracking. Here are some of the benefits for both the participants and planners/producers alike:

- Location information and navigation assistance
- Personalized alerts and welcome letters
- Social networking exchanges
- Capture attendees' movements during exhibit viewing, meetings, social events and then have the ability to market a message based on the movement of each participant. In the moment, you can deliver coupons, discounts or other data that might interest them based on their movements.

These new and upcoming technologies must be used cautiously. Do not invade or spam your participants. Be sure there is inherent value to whatever you send them, or they will turn off or uninstall your app.

Also, watch for firms that will collect all your data and integrate it for their enterprising purposes. When you gather data from your event and each of your participants, treat that data ethically and guard it from misuse of any kind. Watch for hacking loopholes.

Participation vs Attending – Instead of the registrant passively attending a session with a speaker, they will become more involved with their wants, demands, and expect more of an active role in the discussion or presentation. A more interactive environment is the wave of the future (and to a great extent, already here). This is expanding with social media and mobile technology.

Your participants will expect engagement with the speakers, planners and other participants before, during and after your event.

Because of this new way of interacting with everybody involved, rethink your room setups. Instead of a theatre-style set up, set up the room to facilitate discussion and participation.

Social Media and
Social Networking

Using Social Media and Social Networking

Social networking and social media have been the fastest growing innovation to overhaul the events industry in a long time. We are witnessing and participating in a transformation of how we do business going forward. What began as a few unrelated tools for sharing information quickly evolved into a way of life that has profoundly changed the way that we pay attention to, contribute to, become skilled at, and connect to one another.

Today, social media and social networking represent a tremendous opportunity for event-related companies to improve promotion, maintain engagement of clients, reach a larger number of participants, distribute information, network, communicate, share ideas, and offer a better way of learning. These are but a few enhancements social media is currently providing, and it will continue to do so for our industry in the future. The future benefits are still to be discovered.

Up until now, the web-based communication we have been using, Web pages and email for example, have been a one-way form of communication. These new social platforms allow for interaction from all interested parties and can be multi-layered forms of communication in real time. This is a powerful way to enhance engagement from all concerned parties.

As attendees become more comfortable with this new multi-layered communication experience, they are going to start demanding similar experiences from their face-to-face events. Because of this type of networking, our events will begin days or weeks before the actual event takes place and then last for weeks to months after the event is over. The networks that will be created will be with those who attended the event, speakers, entertainers, organizers, and even those who were not able to attend who participated virtually.

Social media and networking gives a new voice to your attendees and allows for a new dimension of communication. Today there is moderate participation in social media among event planners, participants, suppliers and vendors. Those more likely to use a form of social media and networking ranged in age from 18 to 60. We have seen an upswing of Facebook fan pages, Twitter feeds, LinkedIn accounts, Tweetups, hashtags, YouTube viewing and blog contributors over the past five years.

Currently, the top four social networking platforms being utilized are Facebook, Twitter, LinkedIn and Pinterest, and the number of bloggers rises daily. Depending on when you read this section, this information has likely changed. This cultural shift will continue to transform as more people use it. More platforms will emerge, and the popularity of the existing ones will wax and wane. It is not necessarily the platform that is important, but the knowledge of how and why to use that is key.

Beware: With social media, the feedback can be instant and shared with everyone. This real-time feedback is reality. Organizers need to be aware of the conversations going on and be able to turn on a dime during an event when the audience revolts or is discontented with the experience. You should be prepared to adapt your on-site operations to this new reality. No longer do we find out by reading the evaluations that the attendees were not happy. We know right now!

The most popular social sites in 2016 are:

- Facebook
- Twitter
- LinkedIn
- Pinterest
- Google+
- Tumblr
- Instagram
- VK
- Flickr
- Vine
- YouTube
- Snapchat

These change in popularity as time goes by and new ones emerge.

The Roles of Social Media and Networking

Social media cannot duplicate the tactile and sensory experiences available at a live event, but it can — through messaging, video or graphic representations — emulate these attributes. They can never fully replace face-to-face events, but they can create a sense of being there when actual presence is not feasible.

The ability for people to connect with each other online prior to the event can create relationships that are strengthened through the face-to-face meeting. Connections made are not necessarily between people that are attending the event. For example, a Twitter hashtag can connect people that are interested in the content of an event, whether or not any of them ever attend the event. These platforms enable individuals to discuss relevant content and share information before, during and after the event. They will communicate not only on content but will debate a talking point or share their own experience and expertise. It gives a new voice to participants and planners alike and allows for a new breadth of communication.

These practices can benefit event organizers in a number of ways including (but not limited to):

- Brand extension over multiple media sites
- Access to online members, customers and their networks
- Creates the ability to deliver real-time customer service
- Offers collaborative educational programming, advertising, promotion and public relations
- Has the potential to reduce marketing and communication costs
- Creates the opportunities to implement green event practices
- Enhances learning and knowledge retention
- Create new relationships and online communities
- Helps to spread messages across networks in seconds
- Offers affordable education and convenient learning
- Creates peer-to-peer interaction

Social networking is not limited to communication between participants only. You will have the advantage to connect with speakers, read their blogs, and ask questions prior to their presentation. It makes it easier to have a connection with a speaker, especially when the audiences will be large. Speakers can respond either before, during or after their presentation.

You will be able to enrich their experience by understanding how they feel about a speaker, allowing them to ask questions, building on speakers' ideas, and collaborating with others who are listening to the session. We organizers are embracing conversations that are taking place through social media and encouraging attendees to participate in the dialogue.

These terms are used interchangeably but they are quite different. Below is information to help you discover what will be useful to you when setting up your online presence either as an event planner (your brand) or for the event you are producing. Choose which method works best for you.

Social Media is a form of electronic communication where the users create online communities to share information, ideas, podcasts, blogs, personal messages, videos and other content. This strategy is used to create buzz and engagement. This is a one-to-many communication method. Although people can respond and comment to whatever you produce (write, record, create), you own the content. The strategy is deciding how to connect to your audience – blog, newsletter, videos, podcast or e-book.

Social Networking is the creation and maintenance of personal and business relationships online. The strategy is to grow your list of fans and followers. The idea behind the act of social networking seems to be the building of networks of like-minded and influential individuals in a related field or area of interest to gain something of worth that works for both parties involved.

The difference between the two is that social networking involves direct communication and requires conversation from two or more parties. Social media offers channels of our content we put out and a market that content that can be acted upon.

Facebook, Twitter and Pinterest are both social media and social networking platforms (way to engage and a tool) while social media tools are YouTube, LinkedIn, Vimeo and Vine.

	SOCIAL MEDIA	SOCIAL NETWORKING
Goals	Used to generate buzz and interaction. However, you want to increase your bottom line. That means gathering data for lead generation and sales and more.	Ultimate goal is to build your network of fans/followers and nurture those relationships. Once you have social media style, begin using social networking sites like Facebook and Twitter to engage with your audience.
Communication Differences	You are doing the talking, consequently captivating audiences on your site(s). While publishing content, images, videos, e-books, infographics, white papers, etc., you are encouraging active engage-ment with your fans and followers, and ultimately, they will interact with your brand and take action.	There needs to be a mix of both talking and listening. If you're joining groups and networks on social media but doing all the talking (tooting horn, marketing brand, etc.), you're not getting the respect you deserve because you're not listening. You must take time to listen and engage.
Content – a must for both media and networking but in different ways. They can overlap	Try to drive engagement. You need to be posting and sharing images, videos, infographics and other meaningful pieces of your own content to keep your audience engaged and interested in your brand.	You need to have rich conversation, interaction and ask questions. You are having deep, informative conversations with people in hopes of sparking a connection and gaining a new fan or follower while growing your referral network. Engagement creates relationships and builds a following.
Time and Effort	When you have an active social media brand, using tools like Hootsuite or Sprout Social (or others) will save time and measure the analytics. You can create posts and set up a schedule to send them out days later or at regular intervals.	There isn't, as of this writing, a way to automate the way to grow relationships, and you can't cut corners. Each post or interaction needs your attention and focus. Social networking is like dating, it takes time, effort, diligence and patience to make it work.
Return on Investment (ROI) Measurement	The strategy is to generate buzz, excitement, and engagement, and it's hard to boil down the ROI. Over periods of time, you should be able to attribute some type of success, but it is not as easily visible as social networking.	With social networking, if your number of followers continues to increase, that is a measurable ROI.

Event planners should look at how social media can help attendance and bring awareness to all types of events. The example below is old, but take a look at these statistics from 2010. Any popular event today would have increased each number tenfold.

Jon Stewart and Stephen Colbert had a rally in Washington D.C. at the National Mall in November 2010. More than 100,000 people came to *"The Rally to Restore Sanity and/or Fear"* and thousands more watched at home either live or on their DVRs. Social media played a huge part in the success of the event.

A news organization said 215,000 people showed up for the rally. Here are some social media stats:

➥ **Livestream:** There were 570,000 live video streams of the event through Comedy Central or cell phones. Most watched for an average of 37 minutes.

➥ **Sites:** There were more than 800,000 visitors to rally-related sites the day of the event alone across Comedy Central Digital. They had a Meetup.com page where you could find others to watch in your area.

➥ **Twitter:** There were more than 120,000 tweets. Parks Service tweeted that "well over 200,000" were in attendance.

➥ **Foursquare:** An "Epic Swarm" event registered more than 50,000 check-ins and 25,000 badge unlocks.

➥ **Apps:** Within 48 hours, fans downloaded the rally's mobile apps 117,000 times.

➥ **Photos:** More than 35,000 photos from the rally were uploaded within the mobile apps or tagged on Flickr.

➥ **YouTube:** The Rally rolls on with hundreds of thousands of views on many different videos uploaded to YouTube.

Colbert and Stewart understand that they need to thank their online community for getting behind the rally. With all the hilarity and craziness onstage, the message was clear about how you can leverage Social Media to increase awareness and build raving fans for your events and meetings. Maybe not to this extreme, but it is clear social media can help tremendously.

Where to Start

Do you blog, tweet, have a Facebook page, a LinkedIn account, Twitter account, or all of them in one form or another? What platforms are you taking advantage of?

Create and build strategies

Understand who your audience is and what type of interaction you hope to create. What message(s) or participation are you aiming for? Designate a staff or team to work on social media and help implement a budget. Be sure to include guidance to the users on how to use the platform you choose and the rules of conduct. Eventually, document your strategies, policies, procedures, goals and objectives.

Establish goals and objectives

Goals and objectives among event organizers include but are not limited to: increasing attendance, creating an ongoing dialogue with participants, increasing traffic to online properties, obtaining feedback from customers, increasing brand awareness and visibility, getting input for future event content, sharing ideas, developing an online community, and supplementing existing marketing efforts.

Decide your platforms

Make sure your attendees have the means to use the technology then choose the social networking platforms that fit the patterns used by your participants. Typically, LinkedIn is used for business, Facebook for personal communication and Twitter for a mix of the two. Use them all! There are ways to connect platforms so that when you tweet, for example, it is also posted on Facebook. Learn all the tricks of this trade. Designate someone to moderate what people are saying.

Build a following

Event planners can leverage existing databases of attendees, exhibitors and prospects to help build the number of followers on a specific platform. Strategies include sending emails to introduce recipients to the platforms, making content visible to people outside of the database group, and adding multiple layers of media to the social networking platform to generate interest and traffic. Don't forget to reward your most loyal and active followers. Build programs that provide awards such as complimentary event passes, gift cards and other small gifts that will motivate your base to share information with their peers. Sharing builds brand loyalty for the event.

Measure your success

If possible, measure your success. Track what platforms are working and what are not. Use free and paid tools to measure the results. This will help determine if you are meeting your social media goals and objectives.

Face-to-face experiences are more memorable than virtual ones. Extend the life and memory of the event by using social media channels and tools to record a participant's live experience at the event.

Here is an example of what the future looked like just five years ago. Most of these predictions have come to fruition.

The following is "10 ways that I think social media will transform events in the future," by Samuel J. Smith. This article is an excerpt from the FREE ebook *Social Media in Events: 2010*. Download it free!

1)   Attendees will not wait for microphones to ask questions. They will text or tweet those questions as they think of them. Attendees will not wait until the end of a session to ask questions that came up in the first five minutes of the presentation. This does not mean that the speaker has to stop his presentation to answer the questions. Rather, there should be a mechanism to send questions to the speaker in real time.

2)   Attendees will answer questions for the speaker — while she is talking. If the questions for the speaker are streamed through the backchannel, these questions will be available to all attendees. E-learning research tells us that it is very likely that attendees will start answering each other's questions while the speaker (instructor) is still talking.

3)   Attendees will tell you that the speaker stinks, the ice sculpture is melting and the croissants are stale — in real time. With social media, the feedback is instant and can be shared with everyone. You should be prepared to adapt your operations to this new reality.

4)   Attendees will expect to connect with other delegates before, during and after the event. Time is precious. Rather than name tag surf through the crowd, attendees will setup meetings with like-minded delegates before the event. After the event, they will want to keep the conversation going. It will be important that events help them stay connected and translate their face-to-face contacts back into the digital world.

5)   Virtual attendees will start using social media to engage with your content and the on-site face-to-face attendees. Social media and other digital technologies will help virtual attendees join the on-site discussion. They will do this from thousands of miles away. It will be important to make the experience inclusive and collaborative for all attendees.

6)   Attendees will want a voice in the discussion, learning and decision-making process. The gap between the experts that are speaking on stage and the amateurs in the audience has never been smaller. Attendees are well-educated, informed and have information at their fingertips. As this gap continues to shrink, attendees will expect to be part of the discussion, learning and decision-making processes. No more speakers talking and attendees listening!

7) New events will emerge from online communities. It is easier than ever to create an online group, build an audience and start discussions. However, there is still a strong desire for members to meet face-to-face. In 2009, we saw many new events created around Twitter. In the coming years, we will see many more events emerge out of online communities. Equally important, events that do not embrace online communities will be hurt and maybe even close.

8) Attendees will register for your event if their contacts are attending. In the future, knowing if friends or business associates are attending an event will become part of the attendee's decision process. Social media tools that check to see if my LinkedIn connections, Twitter followers or Facebook friends are attending an event already exist. Over time, I think that we will see more of these tools implemented in events.

9) Events will become communities that last for weeks and months rather than a few short days. Event-specific social networks create a social hub where we can start conversations before events and continue them long after the event finished. Creating a social space where attendees can network and discuss trends, hot topics, industry (or business) challenges, and best practices will extend the life of your event.

10) Shareable content will be the way that your event is discovered by new attendees. Your webcasts, webinars, blog posts and whitepapers will need to be interesting, relevant and easy to share. Then, your participants and raving fans will start forwarding, Tweeting and Facebooking this content to their like-minded friends. This will introduce new people to your event and the type of education and thought leadership that you provide. Also, this will make it easier to search and find your event.

Bloggers, tweeters, and podcasters are now a force to be reckoned with. If you are still struggling to understand why you should join in the social revolution, here are some statistics that might persuade you. At the time of this writing, here are some numbers:

- There are slightly more than 3 billion active Internet users (45 percent of the world's Internet users)
- Nearly 2.1 billion people have social media accounts
- 3.65 billion mobile users have access to Internet via smartphones and tablets
- Close to 1.7 billion people have active social media accounts
- There are nearly 1.4 billion Facebook users
- 47 percent of all Internet users are on Facebook
- 4.5 billion likes are generated daily
- Twitter has 284 million active users at last count
- 88 percent of Twitter users are on mobile
- Twitter has 500 million tweets per day
- Google has 363 million users
- The +1 button is hit 5 billion times per day
- Instagram has 300 million users
- 70 million photos and videos are sent daily
- 53 percent of internet users aged 18-29 use Instagram
- 80 percent of Internet users on Pinterest are female
- 70 million users are on Pinterest
- 88 percent purchase a product they pinned
- LinkedIn has 347 million registered members
- Total revenue at the end of 2014 was $643 million (a growth rate of 44 percent over the previous period)
- There are more than 39 million students and recent college graduates on LinkedIn

- Viber has more than 200 million users
- There are 639 million users on Qzone (China)
- There are 600 million users on Whatsapp
- Facebook messenger has 500 million users
- Wechat is close behind with 468 million users (China)
- Snapchat has been valued at close to $20 billion
- Snapchat has 100 million monthly users
- Russia's "VKontake" has 100 million users
- Social networks will earn $8.3 billion from advertising in 2015

These numbers will multiply rapidly as time goes on! You can see how this type of networking can reach an unlimited number of potential customers.

14 TIPS TO INCORPORATE SOCIAL MEDIA INTO EVENT MARKETING

Does your company have a presence at an upcoming trade show or similar event? If so, columnist **Timothy Carter**, Digital Marketing Consultant, (www.timothy-carter.com, @TimothyCarter) has tips for maximizing your event marketing with social media

Social media and event marketing are like peanut butter and jelly – they are great together.

In this digital age, any business not integrating social media marketing into their trade show presence is losing business to their competitors. Social media is an essential marketing channel for event marketers – I don't know about you, but I can't eat a plain peanut butter sandwich.

Following are ideas for using social media before, during and after your event to connect with prospects, deepen relationships with customers, and attract the trade show attendees to your booth.

Generate Pre-Show Buzz

Event Hashtags. Use the trade show's Twitter hashtag. These days, many trade shows and events create a hashtag for the show. Connect with the people who are using that hashtag. Integrate the hashtag into your tweets to promote that you'll be at the show. Be an active participant in conversations surrounding the hashtag.

Company Hashtag. Create a hashtag specific to your company or campaign. Got a contest going on or have a special event? Hashtags are a great way to get visibility leading up to the show in conjunction with the trade show event hashtag.

Host A Special "Happy Hour" Networking Event Or A VIP Dinner. Create a Facebook event leading up to the party. This is a great way to generate some pre-show buzz, as the event page can be shared not just on your company Facebook page but also via Twitter, Google+ and LinkedIn.

Get Media Exposure. Connect with media people in your niche via Twitter or LinkedIn. Get to know them. Share what they're sharing. Comment on their work. Ask them to stop by your booth. Give them a couple story ideas they could write about related to what you're doing. Invite them to your special event.

Teaser Videos. Is your company unveiling new services or products at the event? Have an epic contest you'll be hosting? Teaser videos are a great way to quickly generate interest and can be shared on any social platform. You can upload them to YouTube and even create shorter versions for Vine and Instagram. Share these videos on Facebook and Twitter along with the event hashtag.

Create An Event-Specific Page On Your Website. This page will serve as the home base for all things related to the upcoming show – videos you've created, articles written about your company, sign-up opportunities for that VIP party, and/or other special announcements. It's a great place to direct potential booth visitors to get all the information they want, and you'll gain valuable website metrics and potential leads as they sign up for an event or download a PDF/eBook you could offer.

Social Buzz at The Show

Take Pictures. Give people snapshots of what's happening on the trade show floor (especially at your booth). Pictures of special events, guest speakers or whatever else is taking place at the show keeps your company in the social stream of consciousness.

Get Video Footage Of The Event. Whether it's a short clip of someone participating in a contest, winning a giveaway, giving a presentation or speaking about the event, capturing and sharing moments from the trade show floor gives people who aren't attending a way to experience what's happening at the show. This opens up the opportunity to connect with people without them being there.

Schedule Social Content. Trade shows are incredibly busy. Unless you have a dedicated social member on your team, it's always helpful to schedule out tweets and Facebook posts to supplement your daily engagement activities.

It's especially helpful to tweet out key topics shared about the company, its product(s)/services, and upcoming deadlines for entry into contests or giveaways (if applicable).

Social Giveaways & Contests. Tying your show contest or giveaway in with social media marketing works. It can drive more visitors to your booth. For example, you can have visitors take pictures of themselves with a banner stand that advertises the contest, and they can post the picture to social media – along with the event and company hashtags – as an "entry" into the contest. There are many ways to increase your company's visibility at the show using this method.

Obtain Video Testimonials. If there is a customer who is a huge fan of your company, ask them to record a quick video testimonial that you can share via social media. Have a question or two prepared for them to answer – this keeps them focused and (hopefully) sharing their excitement/passion about your company. A one- or two-minute clip is more than enough. It can be shared via YouTube, Twitter, Facebook and/or your website.

Socializing After the Show

Lead Follow-Up. After the show is over, pour over the list of visitors that connected with you at the show (both in person and on social media) so that you can connect with them on LinkedIn, like their Facebook page and follow them on Twitter. Don't forget to personalize your message to each person. You want to make a genuine connection, not just add them for the sake of adding them to your database.

Post-Show Blogging. It's always a good idea to write about the show experience. You can and should use those pictures, videos, giveaways and contests generated during the show. Recap the reason you were at the show (new products, services, etc.), and thank everyone who participated.

Email! Don't forget to send an email to everyone who visited you at the show (and to those who didn't but may have been invited or wanted to go) to share the recap blog post and include links to all of your social media outposts encouraging them to engage with you there.

These tips were just a few ways to make your next exhibition experience more social. When implementing pre-show social media, marketing and utilizing social media after the show gives your company the opportunity to solidify those connections you made.

Importance of blogging (as an example of a platform)

A blog is a way to speak to an audience on a regular basis in a friendly way. It is sort of a journal of topics selected by the blogger that aim the content at a certain group of interested people. The key is to be constant and have good content.

A blog is the first step in making your event or conference a year-round affair. It can be an essential part of your overall marketing strategy that keeps you in the mind of attendees throughout the year and makes recruiting for the next event easier, faster and actually less expensive. The old rule is true. It costs less in the long run to keep an attendee than to recruit a new one. An event blog will help you recruit attendees and sponsors as well.

Content is the key to keeping your readers and attendees interested and excited so that when you do have a call to action like "Register Now" or "Early bird registration ends tomorrow," your readers are already invested and likely to come on board.

Updating content regularly helps you rank higher with Google and show up more often for different types of search queries. Do not underestimate the power of a blog to drive attendance figures upward. The more people that can find your event, the more people that can attend your event.

A reader is more likely to link to a blog post than your static Web page. Other social media users will come across a blog post and tweet about it, blog about it, email a link to it, or put it on their Facebook or Twitter page.

This shows that using any of the platforms we have mentioned in this chapter can enhance and increase your business. And we want to emphasize that using social media is an ongoing process that begins well before the event starts and may go for months after, or through to your next event.

Going Forward

The future of using social media for events involves more strategy than tools. The industry will continue to see multiple types of social media platforms, each with a unique use and following. Event professionals will continue blogging, tweeting and using Facebook and LinkedIn while other tools emerge. The opportunity is not about mastering a certain tool. It is about developing a process for using social media solutions and strategies to plan for change. As technology evolves, the ability to adapt and take advantage of the tools will define success.

Going forward, social technologies combined with video streaming (live and recorded) and mobile technology will drive change. Social technology will evolve from a networking to a learning tool. Exhibitions and events of the future will be more collaborative, participatory and engaging — with both face-to-face and virtual attendees. Collaboration tools will help facilitate learning. Social media will enable engagement, sustainability and credibility.

Successful sponsors and exhibitors will realize that the old way of selling their products and services has changed. Forward-thinking vendors will recognize the opportunity to engage specific types of customers that perceive value in their products. The online community will self-regulate to correct unacceptable social media behavior, and sponsors and exhibitors who play by the rules — participating instead of promoting — will reap the benefits of their engagement. Sponsors and exhibitors will look to event organizers for networking and social tools to help them identify and engage with attendees in a meaningful way.

As the amount of content grows so will the need to organize and sort the content from conversations, sessions, event organizers, speakers, exhibitors, suppliers and attendees. Knowledge centers will be created for events to allow attendees and others to sort and search. More discussions will take place about who gets access to that content and how much can be given away for free.

Another glimpse into the future includes event innovation workshops that involve networking, learning about new methods of attendee participation, and experimentation with the newest and most innovative social media and learning tools.

Keep a look out for the next best thing because it is either just around the corner or already here and in use by the early adopters. Stay tuned in and connected!

Cover Your Assets –
Contracts, Insurance
and Security

Contracts

It is likely you will be signing different types of contracts during the course of planning at least one of your events. You may sign one for the venue and sleeping rooms, another for food and beverage, one for audiovisual equipment, one for transportation services, one for airline or rental car services, another for your speaker(s) or entertainer(s), another for a tent company, or another for a catering business.

In simple terms, a contract is an understanding of what is expected of each party and instructions on how to resolve problems that arise. They present an opportunity to get some challenging questions answered before the work begins. A contract will set the tone for cooperation and will define the parameters of your ongoing working relationship. Your contract should include a clear work plan with specific deliverables tied to specific dates. A good contract will include much of the following:

- Title
- Brief description of the event
- Brief description of the services or equipment needed

- Detailed list of the services to be provided with projected dates of delivery
- Who is responsible for what parts of the project (contractors, sub-contractors, staff)
- Expectations for communicating the progress of the project
- Payment schedules and amounts
- Clarity on expenses: hourly rates versus fixed pricing
- Ownership of the work products
- How conflicts will be resolved
- How parties can void the contract
- Proper signatures

To protect everyone involved, everything should be confirmed in writing. Contracts have become more detailed and complicated. The days of handshakes and cocktail napkin agreements are long gone. You would be wise to find counsel that is up-to-date on specific contract information.

Contracts are negotiated with the understanding that if your mutual needs and goals are entered into with a mutual commitment, they are created to be fair to both parties. Some may be a simple one- or two-page document, say for a speaker or vendor, or they can be lengthy and complex with comprehensive terms and conditions as with a conference center, hotel, sports stadium or public streets.

Remember to sign the contract as a representative of your company or organization, especially important if you are a hired independent contractor. Sometimes you are the only one, so you must study the fine print before signing.

Everything is negotiable in a contract as long as both parties are in agreement.

Creating a Contract

After two parties have entered into a written agreement (a contract), the terms control their obligations. It is important to get all the commitments written down because if a dispute arises, a judge or arbitrator will require both parties to perform what is in the contract. Oral agreements cannot be enforced. Get it in writing!

The contract typically begins when signed by both parties. The ending date can be changed if it contains a clause stating that the term of the contract can be shortened. The contract should reflect the payment terms. Ideally for the group, no payments should be made until after the program, except a deposit. The contract also should state that final payments are contingent upon receiving a final, itemized invoice from the company.

Amending a Contract

Amending contracts is common practice, but follow appropriate procedures. Avoid handwritten changes if at all possible since they may be difficult to read and may be disputed if they were not properly validated by each party or if it is tricky to tell whether both parties signed after the notes. Legally, they may not be accepted.

If the amendment is small or minor, make notes of the changes in the margins of the contract, initial, and date them. Return the contract so that changes can be included in the next revised version. It is also a good idea to write a cover letter with requested changes listed and a newly amended contract attached. With today's technology, making a fully corrected copy without handwritten changes and signed by both parties is incredibly easy. That is the ideal contract. If changes are significant, an addendum can be incorporated into the contract.

Expect the Unexpected

After a contract becomes valid and binding, a breach of contract occurs if one party cancels or does not fully perform its obligations. The other party is entitled to compensation for losses. Termination of the contract occurs when either or both parties cancel a contract. There are several legal reasons for contract termination. Two common ones are called "act of god" and "force majeure.

Acts of god and force majeure

Hurricanes, wildfires and earthquakes are examples of acts of god and forces majeure, but sometimes the lines are not so defined or obvious. Here are some examples where termination is allowed but damages are expected:

- **A change in economic circumstances**: The banking crisis and the subsequent downturn of the economy and high unemployment were not reasons for termination.
- **Greater expense**: When fewer participants will be attending than previously expected, obligations of contract will require the same amount of money to be expended.
- **Labor issues**: These can be related to strikes, boycotts or picket lines. For example, when Colorado passed anti-gay legislation and when Arizona adopted "papers please," many groups wanted to pull their conferences and conventions. Contracts obliged them to stay or lose in damages. Cancellations are acceptable, yet termination is not. Any venue under contract would have the right to seek damages for a cancellation.

- **Fear of travel:** Threats of terrorism, political upheaval and contagious outbreaks are not a cause for cancellation because they are not forces majeures or acts of god.
- **Threat of anything:** Terrorism and economic or political reasons are not cause for termination.
- They do not fall in either category.

As you can see, lawyers should define contract language about your obligations, but if you do not have a lawyer, here are some issues to watch for and ideas that can save you time and trouble with contracts.

Remember, good contracts protect both parties. Pay close attention to what you are signing. Use these tips and ideas for everyone you deal with and for all contracts you are negotiating.

- Always sign a contract as an agent on behalf of your company or the company that hired you. You do not want to be held personally responsible.
- Look for clearly stated dates, rates, intentions, names, contacts and numbers (hotel rooms, meals, and exhibitors).
- Always read every word in the contract. It is amazing how many people have not read a whole contract before signing it. Do not be penny-wise and pound-foolish.
- Pay attention to cut-off dates. Keep in regular contact with suppliers even after the contract is signed.
- Ask for a clause in the contract that states that any fees not in the contract will not be applicable.
- Never sign a contract unless you agree with it in its entirety. Cross out or edit clauses with which you do not agree, initial them, and get the supplier to initial his or her agreement.

- Make sure that the cancellation clause is reciprocal. Contract offers are inherently one-sided. It is your job to balance it out.
- Specify the dates and times in the contract, i.e.: "The cutoff date for sleeping room reservations is August 14, 2020, at 5 p.m." instead of "The cut-off date is 30 days before the meeting."
- Make sure that all associated fees are stipulated in your contract.
- Include all tax and gratuity percentages in your contract. Understand what they are and how to calculate them.
- Negotiate attrition into your contract for rooms, food and beverage. Ask that attrition be calculated at their profit, not the full rates. If the hotel can pick up the rooms, negotiate that no attrition fee be necessary.
- Cancellation and attrition fees should be based on the meeting site's lost profit not lost revenue. This can be 70 to 80 percent for guest rooms and 30 to 40 percent for food and beverage.

Signing with Vendors and Suppliers

The following guidelines should be taken into consideration when you sign a contract with your vendors and suppliers. You can replace the word hotel or venue with the audiovisual company, the caterer, the tent company, etc.

Conduct preliminary negotiations with the hotel or venue before spending money on a site inspection. Ask to see their typical contract before you visit. Make sure that it meets your requirements, or be prepared to negotiate. Add to the contract any amendment that you want covered for your event. Negotiations can begin early enough that if there is a real problem and a solution is impossible, you will have saved travel time, and your bids will be more accurate.

When dealing with the hotel on any additions to the contract, make sure you are speaking with the person who can make those decisions, but know what you are willing to negotiate and what you will not. Ask for everything, and be prepared to compromise.

Let them know that you are looking at several properties or vendors. They may be more willing to make some deals. If you really want a specific venue, establish a good relationship with the sales staff.

Go over the final contract with your sales person as well as your in-house attorney (of course). Take a few days to sign the contract. If you make changes, try to get an original with all the changes included. Clarity is good! Make sure everything is in writing.

The contract should address which entity is responsible for the safety and security of the audiovisual equipment. Ideally, it should be the audiovisual company. The event planner should not accept responsibility for stolen or damaged equipment.

Privacy concerns

After you have chosen your site, be aware of the policies regarding your participants' information. The last thing you want is your attendees getting unsolicited mail from outside vendors and services because the hotel or venue sold their information. Watch for statements and or clauses in the contract that say that the hotel reserves the right to disseminate the members' information to third parties for any lawful or business purpose, and watch for added provisions to indemnify them from any liabilities resulting from the use of the information.

Sometimes, they may ask for permission that is provided to the federal government for national security purposes. A certain amount of information will have to be released for the vendors and third parties to conduct business, but knowing where the information can be distributed is important. Negotiate in the contract the right to approve all uses of the participants' information.

Signing foreign contracts

U.S. contractual agreements include standard industry assumptions that are not necessarily relevant in other countries. Discuss with the vendors and suppliers those things that we take for granted, such as whether the meeting space in your hotel is free of charge when a certain number of rooms are booked or what a coffee break means in their country. Of course, put everything in writing.

You and the other party must agree on the language and currency you will be using and whose law to use for dispute resolution (yours or theirs). Designating a governing language avoids disputes when different language versions of a contract conflict because of the translation. Choosing an official currency protects the parties against value fluctuations that can affect event pricing. Depending on the country, the court system may be efficient or slow. Without an agreement on which country's laws will apply in a dispute, both sides may try to resolve the matter in their own courts, causing confusion and delay.

There should be a carefully worded clause to cover all unanticipated and unavoidable incidents that would cause cancellation, including civil unrest, terrorism and major airline strikes. Planners should not cede control over declaring a force majeure cancellation to the meeting facility. Local hosts are far less likely to cancel a meeting than the planner. For example, terrorism in the United States would probably not cause a meeting venue in Britain to cancel, but it might prevent the attendees from getting onto the airplane. In situations where there are differing opinions on what constitutes a force majeure, the best option is to create a mechanism for consultation and mediation if a dispute arises.

Insurance

Insurance is an increasing necessity in the world, including for event planning. There are many ways to insure an event. Many of your vendors and suppliers will require you to have insurance and be named on the insurance certificates as additionally insured. And vice versa.

Unfortunately, people are litigious. Events of all kinds face the risk of lawsuits. Planners should understand and protect their events against potential losses and lawsuits by having a basic knowledge of insurance issues affecting them, the organization they work for, and their clients. It is unwise to take the risk of being unprotected. Large and small events are complex financial propositions involving intimidating financial liabilities. Whether you purchase event insurance depends on how important the event is to your corporation financially, what kind of financial risk you are assuming, and the fact that many municipalities and venues will not reserve your space without a certificate of insurance.

The odds of your event's being cancelled are not great, but when something does happen and you have a loss, it will probably be significant. So considering all of the dangers out there, both due to nature and the willful actions of others, you need to secure insurance for your next big meeting or special event.

Type of Event: Luncheon to celebrate a groundbreaking
Duration: 2 hours
Number of Attendees: Booked for 200; set-up for 240
Type of Venue: Construction site for new medical clinic
Subject of Story: One of the hosts murdered during event
Murder weapon: My cream of chicken soup

The event went flawlessly until people lined up to shake hands with the new owners of the land. Then a "disruptive element" arrived. A parent of a patient, a child who had been disfigured accidentally by the doctor, appeared and started a fight with the doctor, repeatedly pushing the doctor's head into my pot of chicken soup. The doctor had his trachea and lungs so badly burned by hot soup that he died on his way to the hospital.

Needless to say, the event was cancelled by the investigating officers, but I did get paid. A big problem was the police held the equipment I had on-site until they finished with the crime scene. The defense attorneys demanded that the banquet remain set until the trial was over.

I was just starting in business and all my serving assets were in that hall, including my folding tables (40), stacking chairs (240), my chafers, utensils, dinnerware, everything. I was essentially out of business until the trial was over. It was only 10 weeks later that they released my equipment. It could have put me out of business.

Solution: My business insurance salesman was my brother-in-law. Before I opened my doors, he insisted I be insured against just about everything, including losing the use of my business assets due to a catastrophic event.

Luckily, all the necessary equipment from the vendors I did business with rained in within five working days. I fulfilled most of my contracts. For a while I had to use the ugliest, cheapest chafers until the manufacturer finally shipped the replacements I ordered — the day before the court released my equipment.

My old on-site equipment became the property of the insurance company, but they sold it back to me for a pittance because they did not want to go to the trouble of auctioning it off. Instead, they came up with a fair price and sold it back to me.

Lesson learned:
1) Always have good insurance.
2) Every knock is a boost. The police and prosecutors ate my food while they did the primary investigation, and afterwards, I got increased business from official county and city events, many weddings, and "Sweet Sixteen" parties for the families of the police department and coroner's staff.
3) No news is bad news: I tripled my catering business within a year. The publicity about a guest drowning in my soup brought the morbidly curious to my doors, which I turned into catering sales by generous samplings of our wares. My retail bakery sales quadrupled.
4) Pick my suppliers more carefully. An equipment vendor who will not produce in an emergency is worthless.
5) Always listen to my brother-in-law.

Dr. Andrew A. Gryffindor IV, PhD.
Retired

Types of Insurance

Insurance companies will consider the type of event you are holding, the number of participants attending, the location, and your level of risk and exposure. For instance, you will pay more for insurance if you are holding a tractor-pull versus a craft show.

There is a public entity type of insurance that covers events such as a group of citizens wanting to hold a July Fourth block party with street closures, a spiritual group holding a service in a public park, or a parade, street fair, sidewalk sale, wedding, or reunion. There is even wedding cancellation insurance.

Look into all of the insurance opportunities, and determine what works best in your situation. Here are some insurance categories that you might need: general liability, event cancellation, promoter liability, participant legal liability coverage, liquor liability, third-party property damage, participant and spectator medical benefits, weather, flood, earthquake, automobile, boiler and machinery, directors and officers, participant legal liability (sporting events only), accidental death and dismemberment, spectator and participant medical, hired and non-owned automobile liability, hired and non-owned automobile physical damage, third party property damage, rental equipment, and unlimited certificates of insurance, including special certificates.

Here is a small list of things that can go wrong and why you should protect yourself. This is not a scare tactic by any means — just a reality check.

- Adverse weather conditions disrupting travel or affecting outdoor activities
- Union strikes causing disruption of travel services or venue staffing and services

- Speakers or entertainers who fail to show for whatever reason
- Venue damage by fire or storm
- Venue not available because the owner double-booked
- The failure of essential production resources such as the power supply
- Terrorism that causes security alerts, disrupting travel or diverting flights
- An outbreak of infectious diseases leading to a quarantine control or restricted travel
- Eruption of civil disorder, revolution, war or other political catastrophes
- Sudden political events such as coups or disputes with other countries causing border closures or withdrawal of visa facilities
- Delay and disruption of travel arrangements. What happens if you have a group stranded at the airport by bad weather? Who pays for the unused food, drink and accommodation?
- Property damage — your own or property belonging to the venue or site
- Loss of enjoyment and motivation — reduction in quality for participants
- Reduced attendance due to some unforeseen event, leading to loss of revenue — potentially devastating for events staged for-profit
- Loss of reputation. It may be necessary to incur expenses to preserve the reputation of the event for next time.

Security Issues

Safety precautions are a serious matter. Global events have increased our need for security, which has touched almost every facet of the event planning process. We now need security for controlling a crowd at a large concert or sporting event, guarding a high-profile person, protecting the personal belongings of the participants, and securing venues or public areas for an event. Today, more than ever, your personal data is also at risk. Security measures are extremely important for protecting your personal information, network and personal computer.

Now we must deal with metal detectors, ID of the tangible and ethereal kind, passwords, personal bodyguards for special guests, and intensive security for large events. Security has always been an event planner's concern, but it was usually a hidden activity. Today, planners are looking to the property's director of security and general manager for guidance and assistance.

The price of security today can come with a hefty price tag. Be sure to budget appropriately.

High-Profile Guests

Prominent figures in our society must take extra precautions, even when stepping out of their front door. When they go to a public event, tight security is required for their safety. Many different types of people fall into the category of "high security" stature. It is best to understand who will need extra security and who does not. If you are not sure, ask them.

When your event includes people who require extra security, hiring the best as well as knowing your role is imperative to everyone's safety.

Celebrities may have their own bodyguards but will expect you to provide some additional security if they are coming to perform. If your event includes celebrity guests, they may be more willing to come if you offer additional on-site security. It is one thing to provide security inside a venue, but you can also provide it for when they are among the crowds outside. Fans can get overly excited and rush the person entering the venue.

Political figures also require extra protection. The level of security required will depend on their stature. Usually, the protection of political figures is handled by the government, but it is important to ask the politician or someone in their office. Remember, when you are working with the Secret Service or the State Department, you are under their orders. If they say they will arrive at this time and enter from this direction, that is what they will do, and you must adhere to their wishes and work with them.

Sports personalities run the same risks as celebrities, and like Hollywood celebrities, they often travel with an entourage and security, but always ask to be on the safe side.

Even private citizens are at risk if they go public with controversial opinions. Adversarial people need protection, too. Know when to hire help.

When high-security public figures have private security staying overnight, take room blocks and assignments into consideration. They may request a suite or several connecting rooms to be blocked off. If this is the case, alert hotel security so that they can work together to build a layout with exits and evacuation plans.

When using a private security company, give them as much advance notice as possible. They will want to do their own survey of the venue and all the streets leading up to it. Security, in some situations, should be left to professionals.

If protests are a possibility; contact local law enforcement. Have medical support on-site for the unexpected. Have a backup plan for all contingencies.

Crowd Control

When crowds are large, it is very likely that security will be necessary. Helping guests feel secure at special events is vital today, and the larger the crowd, the better the security should be. When producing large special events or events with celebrities, do not scrimp on costs associated with security personnel. With that said, communication becomes very critical.

When planning for crowd control or security, take into consideration how many people are expected, the age of the audience, and the reason they are there. Compare a large crowd of 20-somethings gathering for a hip hop concert with a crowd of 30-somethings coming together for a church revival. The security needs will be vastly different. How about alcohol? Will it be served? Will the audience be drinking or doing recreational drugs? These are very important questions, and the answers need to be passed on to security protecting the event.

Striking the right balance between providing enough security and still allowing guests to feel comfortable is the key. Ask yourself what you can do reasonably and appropriately. The likeliness of a terrorist targeting an informal cocktail party at a bar is significantly less than a gala event where the President is the guest of honor. If it is a high-profile event, the highest security measures simply start with not publicly disclosing the location of the event.

Experts agree that uniformed security and undercover security that mixes in with guests are equally important.

If Outside Security Firm is Necessary

Here are some tips for selecting a security company for your event if you need one:

- Ask about what kinds of training its personnel have been through, and any certifications they hold.
- Inquire into their background in event security. Ask for past client names and the type and range of their involvement in past events.
- Ask for references from other clients.
- Ask if the company has ever been sued.
- Do they inspect the venue before the event?

Data Security

Failure to protect personal information can have serious repercussions, including fines and penalties levied by credit card companies as well as lawsuits and damaged reputations. The Sarbanes-Oxley Act (SOX) has created a responsibility for people with access to data to take measures to keep them confidential. Under SOX, that responsibility spreads to outside meeting planners, hotels, convention venues and anyone who handles the data of your participants. Meeting planners can no longer assume that their computers and cyber networks will be safe from information theft. They need to verify that safeguards are in place.

When confidential information exists in an on-site meeting network or in a registration database, it is the planner's responsibility to protect it. To minimize risk and liability, meeting professionals need high standards of due diligence.

Registration and ticket sales data

You must take steps to protect the personal data your attendees will be giving you when registering for your event. When you use online registration, make sure your connection is using the Secure Sockets Layer (SSL) encryption protocol. (The URLs for websites with an SSL connection begin with https instead of http.) The data should be stored in an encrypted, relational database behind a firewall to prevent unauthorized access.

Registration forms, housing lists and other hard copies with confidential information should never be faxed, given freely to staff, volunteers or the venue personnel, or left in the open. Staffers with access to this information should have shredders at their desks.

When a third-party vendor has been hired for on-site registration, do not send the pre-registration database via email. Use a secure File Transfer Protocol site where the file can be downloaded. When you select outside vendors, ask about their data security practices. Decide who is authorized to access the data and how that access is controlled. Be sure the contract includes language that makes it clear that you own the data and that it may not be shared without permission.

Using intelligent data-handling policies and well-designed contracts with third parties can go a long way toward protecting personal registration data. Negligent or careless practices can mean that personal information may be used in unexpected ways or worse, exposed to theft. Privacy policies and practices are not enough to reduce your exposure to risk. When you contract with third parties, include a contract clause that passes along the responsibility for safeguarding confidential information. It can state that "any data that we give you belongs to us and is confidential. You cannot use them for any purpose other than the purpose for which we are giving them to you. When the contract is complete, the data must be returned".

Network Protection

Corporations, organizations, companies and associations spend plenty of money on their own security in their offices. They should request the same level of security when using an off-site venue. When using network access at venues, it is extremely important to have protection from intrusion. It is recommended that you ask your network services provider how the network is protected against denial-of-service attacks and other intrusions. Make sure there is a network operations control center with intrusion detection and incident response capabilities. All network servers should be in a room with restricted access. If you have complex networking needs, bring IT support, or contract a reliable on-site provider.

If security for your participants' computer access is important, do not rely on public wireless access, as it can expose your participants to possible data theft. You can provide a service set identification number (SSID) that restricts access to event participants. For the highest level of security, ask for a Wi-Fi Protected Access-compliant network (WPA) that encrypts the data. To gain access, each user needs a unique password.

Create Your Privacy Policy

A privacy policy tells people how you will use their information. According to TRUSTe, the Federal Trade Commission's Fair Information Practices are the closest thing to a standard for online privacy protection. Based on the principle of full disclosure, they include:

- Notice: Disclose what information is collected and how it will be used. When you collect the information, you must advise the person that their information might be shared and get their permission to do so.
- Choice: Allow people to choose how their information is used. Some people will choose to allow their data to be given and used by third parties, such as hotels or airlines.
- Access: Allow people to review the information once they have disclosed it. This allows them to go back and look at or edit any information given to you.
- Security: Secure personal information so that it stays private.

- Redress: Enable people to resolve any problems that arise. If that information is compromised by a security breach or carelessness, you must notify the people whose information was exposed.

The need for data security does not end when the event ends. Be sure that suppliers return confidential data within a reasonable time. When you no longer need this information, erase it completely. Scrub or wipe your hard drive.

On-Site Logistics

CHAPTER 21

Logistically Speaking

There are dozens of details to handle and tasks to complete in the weeks and months before your event. During that time, winding up all the particulars is a non-stop process requiring good organizational skills. This is the most crucial time involving the timelines and checklists you created and have been following and revising. Get them back out, update them, create more checklists, and assign the ones you have to the appropriate people. Do whatever it takes to get the job done in the most efficient manner.

For example, when you have a good idea of the number of participants coming to your event, relay that number to all involved parties including vendors and suppliers. You will be talking to the venue, caterers, set-up people, decorators, speakers, musicians, security team, volunteers and maybe your participants — all who are involved in the event.

A couple of weeks before the event you should start compiling the event materials, making copies of handouts or putting them into online form, printing name tags, making lists of all kinds, confirming travel and transportation of all parties, boxing and shipping materials to the site, etc. You will be either making your signs or connecting with the sign designers and producers and shipping them, too. Make sure they are on deadline and will get them to the site on time.

Begin making copies of all important paperwork, including your contracts, permits, rooming lists, menus, names and phone numbers of everyone involved. These items will be your reference material and will ultimately go into your binder to share with your assistant or other planners and volunteers. When problems and issues arise — and they will — you will have all the information in one place for reference. The binder should be so organized that if you just handed it off to someone else, that person could run the show without you.

Finalize and Confirm Details

Note: We cannot possibly list everything you need to do in the weeks before your event, but we have listed some important steps in the pages that follow. If you have been making and using your checklists and timelines, you should be way ahead of the game.

The following tasks are geared more towards a business type multi-day or long-day seminar or conference. There will be different tasks to go over for a festival, running race or outdoor event. This is the time to review the checklists and timelines you created and make sure you have the whole event covered. Double check everything.

Registration confirmation

There are many ways registration confirmation can be handled. If you decided early on to purchase a pre-packaged registration software application, confirmations were probably immediately sent to the participants when they registered. If this is the case, download and print the database.

If you did not use a pre-packaged application, you probably entered the names and information into a database. Print out and review the information. This database will be used for sending confirmations, creating name badges and making a participant list. Generate your database in an appropriate program for storing this type of information.

All confirmations should go out as soon as registrations are received to alleviate a mass mailing just before the event. Participants want to know well in advance that they have a confirmed reservation so that they can block the time out in their calendars and begin making travel arrangements and other life preparations that come with leaving home.

Speakers and entertainment confirmation

Confirm with your speakers their needs for audiovisual, room set-up, transportation and any special requirements or requests. Know when they are arriving and how they are getting to the site. Is a volunteer picking them up from the airport, is there a shuttle bus, or will they be taking a cab or renting a car? Make sure their room is reserved at the hotel. Have a copy of their presentation materials. Ask for any last minute changes.

Confirm with your entertainers their needs for audiovisual equipment, staging, and transportation. Know when they are arriving and how they are getting to the site. Will they be needing transportation to the facility or will they arrive on their own? Will they need sleeping rooms? Will they join the group for meals? Ask for any last-minute changes.

Arrange pre-event meeting

Hold a pre-event meeting the day or evening before the event with the facility and staff. Invite all department heads of the facility to this meeting — the general manager, the directors of food and beverage or outside caterer, audiovisual and technology director or outside a/v company, security, housekeeping, banquet room, and even the chef. Invite any other outside vendors if necessary.

Review the event résumé, rooming lists, food and beverage, audiovisual requests, and room set-up. Confirm the set-up of all of your venue space, including each and every room, meal, performance, and the times they are happening. Make sure the rooms are big enough for your latest estimated number of participants, and downsize if necessary (or upgrade if possible). Are the seating arrangements still appropriate and conducive to each particular event?

Go over the audiovisual requirements and food and beverage orders. Find out if your block of hotel rooms is being picked up. If it is not, let go of some of the rooms. If your block has not been filled, you should have released rooms about 60 days ago. But if you have extra rooms and will need to pay for them, use them for meeting space, storage, or to see if you can get upgraded rooms for VIPs.

Discuss any last-minute details or changes. Let them know who has purchasing power within your planning team when additional audiovisual or food is needed at the last minute. Get the cell, pager or extension numbers for everyone at the venue and the hours of their availability. Know whom to call when something breaks, the room is too hot or too cold, or the break food has not been delivered. Go over everything. This may be your last opportunity to get it right!

Finalize transportation needs

Who needs a ride? Are all your airline tickets purchased? Do you need all those buses you hired, or do you need to request more? Who is picking up whom at the airport? Does the hotel shuttle need to run more often because your numbers have increased? Are the limousines confirmed? Check to make sure everything is covered in this department.

Contact vendors and suppliers

If you are using outside vendors, suppliers, and multiple venues and sites, initiate an ongoing dialogue with them as to your needs and wants. As the number of participants increases or decreases, each supplier will need to be informed, whether it is the caterer, the hotel, the bus company or the T-shirt maker. Correct numbers are essential for them to do their job well. If you are ordering flower arrangements for 100 tables and the numbers change so that only 50 tables are needed, the florist needs to know as soon as possible This is true for every item that will be used. It will also reveal any bits and pieces you forgot to order.

Event: Wedding

Lucy is 18 years old and a captain for a catering company. When she and her boss went over the details of the wedding that she would coordinate, the one detail she could not handle was ordering the champagne because she was underage. Her boss said he would take care of it and told her the champagne would be delivered to the bride's father and he would sign for it.

At the reception, the bride's father came up to her and said they were ready for the champagne toast. Lucy went to find the champagne and could not find it. She went to the bride's father and asked if it had been delivered. He said no. Lucy then had to ask her employees if anyone was 21 and if they had a credit card. Luckily enough, one young woman, barely 21 herself, had a credit card. Lucy sent her the local store for champagne. The day was saved. Lucy found out later that her boss forgot to order the champagne. How many 18-year-olds can think that fast? A true event planner!

Jerry, Event Planner
San Francisco

Create event binder

This is a binder for the event planner and any other person who will be working closely with you. It will contain the documents that are the blueprint for the entire event and will be your safety net. You cannot possibly keep all the information in your head. Put it all in one place, your binder, so you know where everyone and everything is at any given moment.

Creating lists for this binder can be a life saver. Make lists of all the hotel or venue personnel whom you will be dealing with, names and positions of your volunteers, how each room should be set up, what audiovisual equipment was ordered for each room, food and beverage orders for all sessions, names and phone numbers of your vendors and suppliers, cell phone numbers of the other organizers, and flight numbers and arrival times of your speakers. Do not forget the list of participants! You cannot have enough lists. Even in today's age of technology, it's a good idea to have a paper list in case something were to happen to your device or you needed something from the Internet and the Wi-Fi was down.

You will also want copies of all contracts, permits, insurance papers, shipping and tracking numbers, emergency procedures, contingency plans, and all other important lists, agendas and timelines. You may want to have a copy of all handouts in case you find yourself making extra copies in the business center five minutes before a session.

> **NOTE:** Have your toolbox nearby at all times. You never know when you will need paper clips, a Swiss army knife, a safety pin or duct tape in a moment's notice. A suggested list of items to pack is in the following pages.

You might want to use ribbons, different color badges, stars or decals for the speakers, VIPs, volunteers or organizers. This is a good way to identify who's who.

Create evaluations forms

Evaluations are a great measuring tool for the success or failure of your event or your speakers. They let you know what parts of your program worked and what needs improvement or deletion. Depending on the scope of your event, you will need one or more evaluation form(s). You can create one to assess the overall event or get more specific and have an evaluation form for each breakout session, speaker, meal or function. They can be very informative if you are asked to do this event again. You can even ask your participants to rate the facility, meals, entertainment, staff and organization of the event. Items such as the marketing materials or the contact with the hosting company can also be included.

Evaluations can be as simple or detailed as you need. If you want a good return of evaluations, keep them short. People tend to be more cooperative if they are short. Allow them to be anonymous, but make room for names and other information if they choose to identify themselves.

The more information you can gather, the better the next event will be. You may find that a speaker was not appropriate, the meals were awful, the music was too loud or the agenda did not make sense. Evaluations can be translated into future profits.

Getting attendees to complete and return their evaluation forms has always been a challenge. To get the best statistical results and a true picture of the event success or failure, you need to get as many forms back as possible. The results will give you the advantage of creating future events that can save you time and money, give you the ability to attract more attendees and best of all, prevent you from future mistakes.

Allow for time to complete the evaluation during the event. Do not wait for the very last minute for the guests to complete the assessments. You may want to email a questionnaire within a week or two following the event or put the form on your website. You will get a great response. Be sure not to wait more than two weeks. You want the event to be fresh in their minds.

Provide a deadline for returning, and then send a reminder a couple of days before that deadline. Remember that people are very busy. Make sure the evaluation forms are designed creatively. Stick to one page, and ask concise

questions. Do a test on the questions with a handful of attendees and colleagues if there is time.

With today's tech-savvy attendees, sending evaluations electronically via email
or a social media site while they are still at the site or shortly thereafter is a
big hit. Most people today have at least one mobile device, a smartphone or
a tablet, and sometimes both. With data accumulated electronically, you can
save an incredible amount of time for processing results. You can also have the
evaluation in an on-site cyber kiosk.

Schedule volunteers

Prepare a staff assignment list including work schedules, times and rules (such
as no eating at the registration desk). You will need staff for a variety of tasks
including working the registration desk, checking meeting rooms for set-up
accuracy, taking tickets at meal functions and checking the audiovisual equipment. Review staff assignments before you go on-site.

Make phone calls, have a meeting and/or send emails or texts to make sure
all your volunteers understand their duties and responsibilities. What will
they be responsible for? What are their shift times? Do they need any more
information from you? Have all of this confirmed before the event; it will save
time and help avoid confusion for both you and the volunteer.

The Event: Celebrity Waiters Luncheon
Purpose: Fundraiser for high school sports
Participants: Local businesses, sports enthusiasts, media personalities, school administrators
Numbers: 1,000 participants, 75 celebrity waiters, five high school bands, five sets of cheerleaders

This was a fast and furious three-hour event. One thousand meals had to be served by inexperienced sports and celebrity personalities. The entertainment included cheerleaders, bands and speeches by local school board members and politicians. I was responsible for a number of tasks that day. One task was assigning jobs and directing volunteers. Well, somehow I overlooked a very large and glaring responsibility. A volunteer to direct the bands! Someone was to meet the buses, direct the band leaders and members to a specific spot and tell them what time they were to play, how long to play and where to march to and from. There were five bands from five different schools with at least 30 members in each band.

I hear through my walkie-talkie, "The first band bus has arrived. Where do I direct them?" It was at that moment that I realized I did not have anyone down there handling this very important task. What did I do? I quickly went through the list of volunteers I had, what their tasks were and when their task started. I was able to pull a volunteer off a task that was not as urgent, someone who could handle this task at the last minute and look prepared. I had the band schedule with me, so I just handed it off to her and off she went. Only she and I knew what had happened.

Nancy C., Events Production
Salt Lake City, Utah

Pack a mobile office

If you are taking your computer, make sure you have all the information and applications saved in case something were to happen to your laptop. Back up all critical PowerPoint presentations or digital photographs. If you are not going to bring your laptop, using a USB memory drive provides an easy way to download, store, and carry your data. Have another copy back at the office with someone who can get you a copy of anything you may need. **Do not forget your smartphone, charger and electric power cord for your laptop.**

Pack your portable toolbox with your office supplies, and pack your office equipment if needed. Put the following items in your toolbox:

Office supplies: Pack a complete assortment of paper, paper clips, note pads, stapler, staples, transparent tape, masking tape, electrical tape, packing tape, duct tape, markers, scissors, batteries, tissues, diskettes, rubber bands, glue, receipt book, correction tape, overnight shipping envelopes and boxes, blades for opening boxes, index cards, Post-its, calculator, flashlight, pens, pencils, clipboards, tools (such as a screwdriver and hammer), transparencies, pens, aspirin, energy bars, bottled water, loose change and dollar bills, tacks, safety pins, extra name tags, whiteout, a few extension cords, and a first-aid kit. Note: I used to say walkie-talkie in this section but with texting and smartphones, walkie-talkies are almost obsolete.

> *"No self-respecting event planner should go*
> *anywhere without a large roll of duct tape."*
> **– Jane G., artist and photographer**

Add whatever else you might need. When you get all these pertinent items in one or two boxes, label them clearly. These are the boxes you will want to open first upon arrival.

Carry a knife or box cutters with you to open your first box. If flying, put it in your luggage. Do not carry it on your person or in your purse. It will be confiscated at the airport. But trust me, have something to open that first box!

Office equipment as needed: A computer, printer, copy/fax machine and associated supplies. The following supplies are cheap insurance: a power protector (get one with a built-in phone-line splitter and snap-on clip for tangle-free phone cord storage), a removable flash card for a camera, a light-weight USB cable, a three-foot-long extended USB cord for various devices, and a hub if several devices will be used at once. For broadband connections for Internet or LAN jack, a portable Ethernet cable cord provides seven feet of cable and will retract into a compact case. If you have purchased audiovisual equipment through a venue or private company, ask them to bring these computer supplies.

Lists: Keep an on-site meeting equipment and supplies checklist in your event binder. Include:

- All the shipping information.
- Original copies of participant packet materials. (You may need to make copies at the last minute.)
- List of names and phone numbers for:
- Organizers, vendors, volunteers with their positions, times and responsibilities
- Site personnel and their phone numbers
- Speaker's arrival and departure times and phone numbers
- Vendors, names, phone numbers and arrival information
- Emergency numbers
- Participants' information and payment history

Like most event planners, I tend to carry too much when I travel. It is confusing, and my shoulder screams at me from the weight of the bag. Of course, the smart thing to do is get the right carry-on bag that can hold all of my equipment and accessories in an organized way.

Event Materials

In meeting situations, conference materials need to be distributed to each participant. If nothing else, there will be name tags, a welcome packet of some kind and an agenda. There also may be some policies that need to be shared: smoking areas, drinking regulations, maps of the venue and cell phone use.

It may be your policy, or it may be the policy of the site. These policies need to be related to the participants somehow, and usually, they are inserted with the welcome material upon registration.

Start gathering, printing and copying the material that will go into the participants' packets. At this point of the planning, you are in the process of collecting speakers' handouts that they will be sharing in their presentation. After all the material is gathered and printed, someone will have to assemble the packets. If the event has 2,000 participants, imagine how long it would take to assemble these packets. This might be a good time to outsource a task. Do not wait until the last minute. There will be plenty of other things to do in the last week!

Remember to take one hard copy of each of the items in your briefcase or carry-on, and save another on your computer. If all else fails, you can take that one handout, agenda or registration form to a local printing or copy center. Some of the most common materials that go in a packet are:

- Agenda and program
- Alphabetical attendee list (with or without full address info)
- Coupons
- Evaluation forms (overall and specific session)
- Facility map if not included in program
- Giveaways (promotional gifts)
- Invitations to special events
- Last-minute information not in the program
- Local maps, brochures or magazines
- Name badge
- Meal or event tickets
- Receipts
- Ribbons
- Special handouts
- Tickets
- Welcome letters or introduction letters

As a presenter, the hardest thing to hear from a meeting planner is they didn't get your PowerPoint presentation and didn't complete the handouts. I arrived to one speaking engagement and both these things happened. All items had been sent to the meeting planner way in advance. Well, backups are always important. I had a memory stick so that was amazing. Plus my assistant was able to quickly re-email the presentation. There was an onsite fed ex and they completed the handouts in less than one hour. The truth is, had we not done some pre checking with the meeting planner, we would not have known all this was missing! I arrived early to ask the right questions. She stayed calm and so did I. However, I realized how important it is to establish good relationships with the planners! This was not easy and she admitted to not being organized since she was sent all the items she needed way in advance. So when things happen, everyone breathe! See what actions can be taken to save the day. Another time I had to forgo the PowerPoint since she didn't have it and I forgot my memory stick. It was still a great presentation! Be prepared no matter what and be kind and respectful no matter what!

Jill Lublin, 3x international bestselling author
and speaker, JillLublin.com

Create name badges

One of the most important and noticed items at an event are name badges. The badges provide introduction and promote networking. Make sure they include name, organization, city and state. You should be able to get this information from the database you created when the participants registered.

Make them readable. Add the logo, use color and make different type sizes, depending on your needs. There are many options for the size and type of paper that can be printed as well as several different holder styles. You can print the badges yourself or have them done professionally.

Shipping

When you are ready to pack and ship materials, there are many issues to consider so that you can easily track each item. The better organized you are, the better you can help the shipper find the right (lost) box. More importantly, you know exactly what is inside each box.

First, create an organized system for the inventory that goes into the boxes and organize the boxes themselves. Clearly record what is placed in each box, and clearly identify the box on the outside with a numbered system so that you will know exactly what is in box "P1 of 5." For example, use the letter P for your personal items, such as your tool box, lists of important documents and shipping labels. You may want to use H1 for the presenters' handouts. If you have 10 boxes of handouts, your numbering systems would be "H1 of 10," "H2 of 10," and so on.

Create a system that works for you. Label all boxes using the same format. Keep an inventory list of what is in each box, how that box is labeled and what type of box it is, and take it with you to the destination in your briefcase. Make copies of the list and give them to others on your staff. If a box is missing, you will know exactly which box and what it contains. This may sound like a lot of work, but when your carrier tells you that only nine of the ten pieces have arrived, you will know exactly what is missing. You can assist the carrier by saying it is a blue plastic bin with the numbers P5 printed in large red letters on the side.

On the same inventory list, include each tracking number for each box as well as phone numbers of the carriers.

Make sure you give yourself plenty of time to get boxes shipped. It can get very expensive if you have to quickly ship materials that weigh 30 pounds per box. Do not send the boxes too early either as you may be charged a storage fee at the facility.

Sometimes your vendors or sponsors will be shipping materials to your event. Before you leave your office, call your vendors, and confirm that they have sent shipments and get all shipping information from them. Get the tracking numbers, shipper's name, address, the date shipped, how many boxes to expect and the weight.

Also call the site or venue, and confirm whether they have received your shipments. The sooner you know that a box is missing, the faster you can find it or replace it. When you are getting confirmation of the piece count, ask the consignee (recipient) to count the pieces that are in their storage or warehouse rather than read it off a bill of lading. If you do not disclose how many pieces there are supposed to be, there is a higher likelihood that they will actually count the pieces. Looking for missing items on-site is very time-consuming, and if important materials are missing, it can have a severe impact on the event.

If you are shipping to the hotel before your arrival, ensure that the consignee will accept your materials and store them for you. Find out what they will charge for this service. Ask them to check the freight for damages or shortages before they sign the bill of lading. Know whether there are any national holidays in the days and weeks before your event. Holidays can slow the supply chain from warehousing, trucking and customs. Working hours — particularly with customs — can be different in the country of destination. Know what you are up against when planning your shipment.

Bring preprinted, overnight shipping labels to the event for returning your unused materials and personal items. These are very handy when you need to ship your leftover materials back to the office. Remember to remove any old labels from the boxes before you apply new labels. Old ones have electronic bar codes and can be scanned unintentionally.

CHECK, CHECK, AND DOUBLE CHECK

I arrived in Minneapolis at the hotel a couple days before our week-long inten-sive was to begin. I always try to arrive early to meet with the venue staff, get the lay of the land and to make sure all our materials arrived. When doing my regular check of the boxes shipped, I discovered that a couple boxes of important handouts did not arrive. Fortunately, I had the originals with me, and I quickly found the nearest copy shop and frantically made enough copies. I always travel with a complete set of handouts for this very reason.

A day into this same training, we realized that a few boxes from our video vendor at the California Department of Education had yet to arrive. We had them tracked through UPS confirming that the boxes had been delivered to the site. The hotel could not find them. Again, we asked the hotel to look for them to no avail. On our last day there I mentioned that each box of videos was worth around $1,200. That seemed to do the trick, and all of a sudden, they appeared. Since then, we are very consistent about having tracking numbers with us and pressing the hotel to search for boxes until they find them.

Karla Nygaard, Conference Coordinator
Sausalito, CA

Shipping tips

Each piece should have two shipping labels because labels can be mistakenly turned inward, placed out of sight or fall off. When shipments are stacked, your labels may face inside the pallet and be invisible. Two labels are especially helpful when a piece is missing and the warehouse is searching for it. Two labels increase the chances that people will read them.

Using boxes with strong corners decreases the chances of their falling apart in transit. Strengthen the box with packing tape on all the edges and corners. Remember that corners of boxes will crease. Try plastic containers instead of boxes. Corners will not dent, and they stack better. Most have handles, making them easier to move around.

Out of country shipping

When your event is in another country, shipping material becomes challenging. Since each country has unique customs requirements, it is vital to choose a good customs broker, one who is knowledgeable in the country where you will be exporting your goods. Choose a broker who has experience in working with trade shows, conferences, events, sporting events, musical and theatrical performances, and exhibitions. A knowledgeable customs broker can ensure that your goods clear customs and also minimize duties, taxes and other related fees.

Customs delays of days, or even hours, can mean the difference between having your material at your event and having nothing. Events are scheduled to move in or out after hours and on weekends and even through holidays, requiring your broker to work those same nonstandard hours. Be sure the broker you choose is willing to work on your schedule.

One of the challenges is to understand the rates and charges. Make sure you have in writing what the door-to-door costs will be, including any applicable duties and taxes. Understand that you are importing goods to another country and will be dealing with bureaucratic red tape. Allow plenty of time.

The Day Has Arrived!

Lights, camera, action! Are you ready for show time? If you followed the timelines, checklists and everything else that has been suggested to you in this book, you should be prepared for action. This section helps you with the finishing touches and tells you what to do when you arrive at the event site. We will walk you through the process, including checking into the facility, setting up your office, getting acquainted with the facility staff and setting up your registration area. We also have tips on what to do while the event is going on. Know this: You will be extremely busy. Wear comfortable shoes and clothing.

When You Arrive

When the event is large, try to arrive a day or two before it begins to give yourself time to establish a presence and get comfortable with the surroundings. Have the pre-planning meeting with the sales manager, catering manager, audiovisual department, the general manager and all other important players as soon as possible. Go over all the details. Make any necessary changes during this meeting. Introduce the facility members to any members of your team who are authorized to make decisions in case you are unavailable. Let them know who is allowed to order more coffee at the breaks, charge that last-minute order for an extra easel, or print 50 extra handouts.

Establish a chain of command for implementing changes or handling emergencies, and communicate it to the facility and to your staff. Review the list of names, cell numbers or extensions, and time schedules to know who will be where when. You will want to know if there is a shift change in the middle of your event and if so, when that happens and who is in charge.

Check to see if your equipment, supplies and materials have arrived. Check them yourself if you can, and compare them with your lists. This is important because if there a box is missing, you will have time to hunt it down.

Walk around the site, and familiarize yourself with the layout. Get familiar with the hotel staff. Introduce yourself to the front desk personnel. Get to know people by name. Make friends. You will be glad you did.

Set up your office space, unpack and get organized. Use a dedicated room throughout the event if possible. It could be your sleeping quarters or the registration area. Nonetheless, get started setting up your area.

Hang banners, and set up signs if the facility will allow. Get directions to the closest copying service, florist, office supply, grocery store and local caterer. You may need them at a moment's notice. Do as much as you can the day before the event.

If you cannot be at the site before the day of the event, organize yourself enough so that when you do arrive, you can hit the ground running. Make sure that all of your staff is prepared to do the same. If you are meeting the caterers that morning, have your checklist ready to check off equipment and do the same with the tent company, electricians, musicians and florist. Your agenda should display when the suppliers and vendors are to arrive and what they are responsible for bringing.

Event: All-day workshop for 200 Health Professionals
Venue: Church auditorium with side room for continental breakfast and registration

This was the 15th workshop held in this city and specific venue. At each workshop, we served muffins and coffee during the registration at 8:15 a.m. There were particular muffins that we ordered and served, and they were special enough that we mentioned them in our marketing material. They were the healthy variety and had been a hit among past attendees. For previous events, the delivery person (same person, same bakery) would come to the venue between 7 and 7:30 a.m. to drop off dozens of boxes. We always made sure there was plenty of time between the delivery and setting up the registration area. This particular morning, the delivery person dropped off the boxes without getting a signature because that is how it worked in the past. All the boxes were labeled with the name of the event and the correct address.

One of the volunteers was hungry and decided to have a muffin. As she opened one of the boxes, to her great surprise, there were no muffins but thousands of frozen French fries. Oh no. No one at the meeting had the phone number of the bakery! We quickly gathered, put all of our money together and sent a couple of the volunteers down to the closest grocery store for fruit you can eat with your hands.

We needed finger foods because we had plates but no forks. So the morning was saved! The attendees received at least some food as promised. The speaker made note of the story and was able to make light of the situation.

Lesson learned:
- ➡ Look inside all deliveries.
- ➡ Have someone specifically assigned to receive and sign for the delivery.
- ➡ Keep all important phone numbers on hand.
- ➡ Know your alternate food sources within a five-to-10-minute range of your venue.

Judith Shaw, Coordinator
Bolinas, CA

Rehearsal

The rehearsal can be done up to a week before the event when possible, though the day before is usually when you get the opportunity because you will be at the site. It will be a dry run of the agenda. It should be done with as many of the staff and volunteers as possible. The rehearsal gives you the opportunity to work out any logistical issues, confirm procedures and clear up any unanswered questions. Sometimes, there will not be time for a rehearsal, but when there is, here are some details you may want to check.

- Is the registration area designed for easy flow of traffic?
- Is the help desk situated in a focal nearby area?
- Do we have all the appropriate supplies and signs?
- Are there stairs leading to the stage that might be a problem for the speakers?
- Is there enough room between tables and chairs for traffic to flow?
- Is the room set up so that everyone can see the stage?
- Have all the signs, lists and agendas been given to the appropriate people?

Registration Check-in Area

Registration is where most attendees, exhibitors, vendors, speakers and facility staff will go to pick up materials, ask questions and get help. Therefore, it is important to have someone there at all times who can make decisions and answer questions. Remember that your registration staff will be busy. Any questions your staff cannot answer should be referred quickly to someone who can help. If you cannot have the "answer person" remain in the registration area (maybe because it is you and you have to be everywhere), make sure your staff members have smartphones to be able to reach you instantly.

If you have hundreds of registrants, ticket holders or guests (each with an individual registration packet), you may need a large check-in area with registration booths instead of tables and chairs. How you set up registration depends on what kind of materials you are providing. For example, assume all the registration packets contain the same info, and the only unique item is the participant's name badge. Here, you can place the name badges in alphabetical order on tables. As the participants pick up a name badge, you check off their name and hand them a packet. Done! If the packets are different for each individual, they should be placed in alphabetical order behind registration. If the group is large, break up the registration stations alphabetically, A–F, G–L, M–R, S–Z, for example.

Registration stations and staffing are very critical. Consider the number of participants you will have and break up the registration so that traffic flows easily. Plan for at least one staff person for every 75 participants.

For larger conferences, greeters are a good idea to assist and direct people in getting around the meeting site. Send arriving exhibitors and speakers to different areas, and provide them with special assistance geared to their needs.

It is good to have a specific area for money-related issues with a designated troubleshooter who knows all the ropes and can solve any problem or issue that will arise.

Remember that the majority of guests will arrive about the same time. Be prepared for them to get what they need and move on. Even if they are coming to a party without a necessary check-in point, keeping them from clogging the entry way is crucial. Do not have the bar or appetizers right inside the entry door. Move the people toward the back of the room when possible.

Signs

Use signs to give your participants directions. Direct them to the bathrooms, registration areas or anywhere that something pertaining to the event is happening. Let them know where to find the book sellers, exhibits, excursion sign-up, transportation information, lost and found, rest rooms, phones, etc.

Give them as much directional information as possible. Do not make them ask. The easier it is for the participant to move around the event, the better the traffic flow will be, and the less will be asked of you and your staff.

Be as clear as possible with your signs. Make your signs are at least eight feet off the floor for visibility. Be sure they are appropriate for the event.

On-Site Management

Magic can occur if you are well organized. Remember, plan for the best outcome, but be prepared for the unexpected and remain calm.

Staff and volunteers

Volunteers and staff may be the first encounter for your participants. Whatever you do, keep your staff and volunteers happy.

Make sure you have enough volunteers and they are prepared to greet the participants. Arm them with enough information to answer all questions or to point them to someone who can. Make sure they have all the materials needed to register the participants and be of assistance.

You may want one person to be responsible for all the volunteers. This person not only shows them what they need to do, but he or she can bring them water and snacks, too. Train your staff:

- To wear an attitude that is truly welcoming to everyone.
- To be prepared to solve problems.
- To be comfortable and professional.
- To be willing to replace another position in case of an emergency or bathroom break.
- To smile at all times.

Another handy thing to have is a list of frequently asked questions by attendees. Brainstorm with staff and key volunteers in advance to identify the questions you think attendees will ask your registration desk personnel, and list the answers. Here are some typical questions:

- Where are the bathrooms?
- How can I pay for the event?
- Can I pay by check or credit card? Which ones do you accept? Where is the nearest bank or ATM?
- Where are the meeting rooms? Have your staff become familiar with the floor plan?
- I need to cancel the last day. Can I get a refund?
- I have a special meal request. Whom do I tell?
- Is Suzie Q. registered for the conference? Has she checked in yet? Can I leave a message for her?
- Where can I get breakfast, lunch or dinner?

Also, it is essential that you train your staff on the emergency procedures of the hotel. They should know what to do in the event of any crisis. Make sure you know the facility's emergency procedures and communicate them to your entire staff.

Inspect the rooms

Have someone inspect each room at least 30 minutes before a session begins if possible. See that the room set-up is correct and the audiovisual equipment is there and working! There is nothing worse than having a speaker begin talking into a microphone that is not working or emitting a loud squeal. We have all experienced that sound and would be happy to not have to hear it again.

Know where the lights and thermostats are in every room. Rooms should be cool in the morning because after people arrive, the room will warm up. Do not rush in turning up the heat. Hot rooms create sleepy participants.

Do not depend on the hotel staff to prepare the rooms fully. Check each room yourself or have volunteers for the job. Just check them out! Inspect the rooms after the event is over. Participants may have left belongings behind.

Do the same for your refreshment breaks. Make sure they are set up on time and there is the correct amount of each item you ordered. Is the coffee hot enough? Were there enough cookies? You would be surprised how this simple order can go wrong. You do not want your sessions to break when the refreshment station is not completely set up or to have the food or beverage run out before all participants have had the chance to indulge.

This also applies to any food and beverage function such as receptions, buffet dining, and mid-morning and mid-afternoon breaks.

At the end of the day

Get the master bill from the facility and review it while everything is still fresh in your mind. Go over all charges. Make changes immediately if needed. If your event is longer than one day, doing a review every day will save you from having to remember what went on two or three days ago. Mark up the statement, and speak with someone right away. You can also go over the number of items that you were short or ran out of early and adjust the numbers for the next day. Before you retire, review tomorrow's function sheets with the appropriate site managers.

Contingency Plan

No event, no matter how well-planned and well-run, is immune from an occasional calamity or crisis. Problems can arise in any area anytime, anywhere, and as planners, we need to be prepared. They can be small, such as boxes not arriving on time, or large, such as full-blown disasters like fires, hurricanes and earthquakes. Even the threat of terrorism or other health-related scares can arise in a moment's notice. You cannot possibly plan for all situations, but a good event planner must have a contingency and emergency plan in place. Your event site should already have an existing plan. Ask to have a copy, and spend some time going over it with your staff and volunteers. Better safe than sorry.

There is the plan for the day-of-the-event emergency, and then there is a big-picture, contingency plan for the large-scale, totally uncontrollable occurrences, such as natural disasters, political unrest in a particular area of the globe, or even health scares that can change things weeks or months before the event. Always plan for the unexpected.

If your event is outside, do you have a contingency plan for bad weather? What will you do with 500 people when it is raining in the middle of July and the picnic grounds you have rented have hundreds of puddles?

What do you do when you get a phone call from your keynote speaker the day before the event saying she has laryngitis? What will you do when the caterer is two hours late for a sit-down reception for 200? What happens to your event when there is a major traffic jam and half your participants will not arrive on time or at all?

I went to El Salvador for a conference that was scheduled during the broadcast of the World Cup. I was given a time to speak because my company was the marquee sponsor. Unfortunately, at the exact same time I was scheduled to start my session, Japan was playing Brazil and, not surprisingly, no one showed up for my session. The event planners were red-faced and apologetic, and I was slightly embarrassed.

They ended up rescheduling my session for the next day, but I only had 15 minutes to speak during breakfast. Not everyone showed up, and I was only able to present a quarter of my material.

The moral of this story is to make sure you understand the priorities of a foreign culture before you create your agenda. Always plan for last-minute changes due to uncontrollable circumstances.

Ingrid

Part of being an event planner is the ability to think on your feet and come up with alternatives and quick fixes. Always be prepared!

- Develop an emergency plan before arriving on-site. When the event is large, take time to put your plans into writing, increasing the chances that everyone will follow it in the event of a crisis.
- Review your insurance coverage before your event. It is likely that your insurance needs may be different from year to year depending on the venue you are using and the types of activities included in your meeting.
- Hire emergency medical technicians to work on-site at your event. Make sure they will be available throughout the event and that all staff members know how to reach them.
- Communicate safety information to attendees. Consider providing safety tips and emergency procedures in individual registration packets.
- Stock your staff office with emergency gear. Some important items to keep on hand include a first-aid kit, a weather radio and an attendee list with emergency contacts. Some planners even print emergency contact information on the backs of attendee name badges.

Planners need to be ready for different challenges today, such as new technology, changing personnel, changing demographics of your participants, economic downturns or upswings, labor issues, needs and wants of the public, and the increasing globalization of just about everything. Although these may not be considered emergencies, they are issues that you must take into consideration and be prepared for. If you have spent a great deal of money setting up an event in Hawaii for a week-long conference and the economy takes a turn for the worse in your industry, what are your backup plans? What if the airline mechanics go on strike that week or your largest group of participants gets laid off because the company CEO was caught embezzling? These things do happen.

Event: Holiday Party
Company Employees and guests: 350

Two days before a large company holiday party at an elegant, private mansion in the Buckhead area of Atlanta, the home burned to the ground. In less than one day, I had to find another location and alert everyone involved.

Because I had so many contacts in Atlanta, I started calling, begging for assistance. It was the holidays in the city, and if you do not book a venue early, you are either out of luck or will get the bottom of the barrel for choices.

Tenacity prevailed and a mansion not far from the original spot was found, but that meant getting new decorations, re-arranging parking and revisiting site plans. They now would need valets because the new site had no public parking. Buses had to be rented and positioned at the old site to transport guests back and forth to the new site.

Because I was quick on the draw and had hundreds of contacts in the city, I was able to pull off the party while hardly disturbing the flow of the event or the participants. It was fortunate that the company had money to pick up the extra costs and wanted to have the show go on.

Linda D., Event Planner
Atlanta, Georgia

Wrap It Up!

The last participant has departed, the volunteers and staff are gone, and the show is over! Take a deep breath, and congratulate yourself. If you remained calm and serene with a smile on your face, no one knows what actually went on behind the scenes. The participants probably did not even notice all the last-minute changes, substitutions or near mistakes.

Tying up loose ends, like paying bills and generating reports, is the final task of your event. Pre-arrange a debriefing meeting with everyone involved to review the event within the following week so that it is still fresh in everyone's mind. Be sure to make an extensive thank-you list and begin the appreciation process. Follow up on the evaluation forms you requested from your participants, and start cataloging your event. All of this information will be incredibly valuable for your next event. Do not reinvent the wheel or make the same mistakes next time. No event will be exactly the same, but the information will be priceless.

Was your purpose realized? Did the event make money, lose money or just break even? Did you achieve your return on investment goals, your financial goals? What did you like or not like about each aspect of the event? The questions and answers will guide you to keep certain characteristics and discard others.

Pay the Bills

To alleviate problems with the final bill, it is recommended that if your event is longer than one day, you review all charges at the end of each day. When it comes to the end of the event, you will be ahead of the master bill reviewing process. In some cases, your master bill will come well after the meeting is over. Keep daily accounts of your charges, and go over your contract to make sure both you and the vendor have met your obligations. Also look for last-minute additions to your bill such as shipping, food and beverage, or audiovisual charges. If your event was large, it is more than likely there will be an error on the master bill. Always double check!

Get copies of the final report from the facility including how many rooms were booked, all the numbers of food and beverages, and audiovisual usage. If possible, find out how participants used facilities such as restaurants, pools and spas, and room service. This information will be helpful if you repeat the event next month or next year.

Debriefing

Everyone who participated in the decision-making and planning stages of the event should attend the debriefing meeting if possible. This is an opportunity to go over the things that went right and the things that need improvement. Please do not use this meeting to do any blaming. What's done is done. Move on and take appropriate steps to ensure that it does not happen next time.

Come up with additional questions specific to your event. Some questions you might cover:

- What worked? What did not?
- What would we do differently next time?
- Were your goals and objectives met?
- Did you realize your defined purpose?
- Did you come in on budget? Did you spend more in one area than anticipated? Why?
- What unanticipated expenditures did we have? Were they necessary?
- Did your participants seem to enjoy certain aspects over others?
- Were the speakers or entertainment appropriate?
- Was the food appropriate?
- Were the lighting, staging and sound right?

Thank You's

Say "thank you" to everyone, and do it soon after the event. Be specific! When appropriate, put your thank you's in the form of a letter. In some cases, a phone call or email will suffice. Some very helpful people are warranted a gift of some kind. It does not have to be expensive, just thoughtful. Do not hold back in the area of appreciation. Especially thank all of your volunteers. Many people worked very hard to make your event successful. Make sure they know how much they meant to that success. Do not forget your vendors. They also need to know that their services and personnel did a good job. Remember, you will need them next time!

Evaluations

Tabulate the evaluations right away before you move on to your next project. They provide important information that you can use for your future events. Prepare an organized summation to include some of your personal interpretations and recommendations. Disperse the summation to all the decision-makers and planners that were involved.

If you had separate evaluations for each speaker, provide them with a copy of their evaluations, and keep a copy for your records.

Final Report

Create a final report, and include everything. This just means consolidating all the information into one place. The information is used to track your history and will be used for future events.

Put at least the following information in your report:

- Event name, dates and location
- Goals and objectives — defined purpose
- Number of participants — paid
- Number of participants — complimentary (VIPs, sponsors, staff and cancellations)
- The facility report with the number of rooms, food and beverage
- Evaluation summation
- Any conclusions you made from the debriefing meeting
- Copies of all marketing material
- Copies of all handouts and agendas
- Your timelines and checklists

- Budget estimate and all final costs
- List of all volunteers and staff
- Record your suppliers — include phone number, key information and any evaluation you have of them. You may want to use them again.
- Evaluations
- Copies of all invoices

Now go reward yourself for a job well done!!

Resources

There are thousands of companies, corporations, associations and industries that supply information to assist you in performing your job. Listed here are names and websites for your convenience. Surf the Internet and find many more. They change constantly!

At the print date of this book, all web addresses were working. Some will already be out of date by the time you log on. We apologize if that happens. Just because they are listed here, we do not personally recommend or endorse a product, service, vendor or organization. This is just a service to you. Go ahead and search for others. They are out there! And do your own due diligence if you choose to work with any of these resources.

ASSOCIATIONS AND ORGANIZATIONS	
ahla.com	American Hotel and Lodging Association
amanet.org	American Management Association
asaenet.org	American Society of Association Executives
ascap.com	American Society of Composers, Authors, and Publishers
td.org	Association for Talent Development
asta.org	American Society of Travel Agents

acced-i.org	Assoc. of Collegiate Conferences and Events Directors – Int'l
acte.org	Assoc. of Corporate Travel Executives
nsfre.org	Assoc. of Fundraising Professionals
bbb.org	Better Business Bureau
bmi.com	Broadcast Music, Inc.
canspep.ca	Canadian Society of Professional Event Planners
cemaonline.com	Corporate Event Marketing Association
cimpa.org	Connected International Meeting Professionals Association
conventionindustry.org	Convention Industry Council
Eventplannersassociation.com	Association with current trends, ideas and statics
hsmai.org	Hospitality Sales and Marketing Association International
iacconline.org	International Association of Conference Centers
destinationmarketing.org	Destination Marketing Assoc. Int'l (formerly known as International Association of Convention and Visitors Bureaus)
iahmp.org	International Association of Hispanic Meeting Professionals
ialep.org	International Association of Law Enforcement Planners
iasbweb.org	International Association of Speakers Bureaus
iccaworld.com	International Congress and Convention Association
ifea.com	International Festivals and Events Association
ismp-assoc.org	International Society of Meeting Planners
ises.com	International Special Events Society
mpiweb.org	Meeting Professionals International
nsaspeaker.org	National Speakers Association
ncbmp.com	National Coalition of Black Meeting Planners
pcma.org	Professional Convention Management Association
sesac.com	Performing Rights Organization for Songwriters and Publishers
sgmp.org	Society of Government Meeting Professionals
ufi.org	Global Association of the Exhibition Industry

INDUSTRY JOBS	
coachfederation.org	International Coach Federation
hcareers.com	Hospitality Careers
meetingjobs.com	MPI Jobs and Community
nace.net	National Association for Catering and Events
searchwide.com	SearchWide Executive Recruitment Experts
CERTIFICATIONS AND ACCREDITATIONS	
conventionindustry.org	Convention Industry Council (CIC)
hsmai.org	Certified Hospitality Marketing Executive (CHME)
www.iavm.org/cfe/cfe-overview	Certified Facilities Executive (CFE)
ises.com	Certified Special Events Professional (CSEP)
mpiweb.org	Certificate in Meeting Management
nace.net	Certified Professional Catering Executive (CPCE)
nsaspeaker.org	Certified Speaking Professional (CSP)
site-intl.org	Certified Incentive and Travel Executive (CITE)
MEETING AND EVENT MANAGEMENT RESOURCES	
hotels.com	Hotels – 50,000 properties worldwide
experient-inc.com	Event Services
eventplannersassociation.com	EPA Event Planners Association – current trends, ideas and statics
meetingapps.com	500 apps divided into 25 categories
meetingsnet.com	Meeting Planners Survival Guide
officequest.com	Preferred Club Virtual offices
jilllublin.com	Publicity and public relations guru
plasa.org	Worldwide technical resources for the entertainment industries
pmpn.com	Professional Meeting Planners Network
shindigz.com	Shindigz (Special theme kits)
seatguru.com	Airline Seating
www.keyspeakers.com/	Your one stop resource for great speakers
successfuleventplanning.com	Event Services /Author's website

ticketleap.com	Ticket Service for $100 or less per month
ustravel.org	US Travel Association
uniquevenues.com	Guide to Unique Meeting & Event Facilities
zagat.com	Hotel, Restaurant, venue reviews
MEETING TECHNOLOGY SOFTWARE	
123signup.com	Online Registration
cvent.com	Event and emarketing
emssoftware.com	Event Management Systems
certain.com	Enterprise Event Management Software Solution
eventregistration.com	Cyber Guide to Event Promotion
evite.com	Online invitations
expocad.com	Exhibit floor design
meetingmatrix.com	Event Design
mpoint.com	RFP Wizard
netsimplicity.net	Meeting Room Scheduling
newmarketinc.com	Marketing Design Management
passkey.com	Passkey.com – empowers meeting planners
pcnametag.com	Event products
perfecttbableplan.com	Table planning
Lanyon.com	Event registration
WEBCONFERENCING	
gotomeeting.com	Online Meetings made easy
on24.com	Virtual environments
freeconference.com	Conference Calls
intercall.com	Global Conferencing solutions
readytalk.com	Audio and Video Web Conferencing
SOCIAL MEDIA MANAGEMENT TOOLS	
hootsuite.com	Ability to manage multiple social media sites from one location
tweetdeck.com	Same as above
socialoomph.com	Same as above

cotweet.com	Same as above
ifttt.com	Same as above
twitterfeed.com	Same as above
spredfast.com	Same as above
buffer.com	Same as above
socialflow.com	Same as above
sproutsocial.com	Same as above
TRADE PUBLICATIONS	
btnonline.com	Business Travel News
bizbash.com	Biz Bash online (Event Planning News, Ideas and Resources)
meetings-conventions.com	Meetings and Conventions
Meetingfocus.com	Meeting and event current information
chiefmarketer.com/	Promotion and Marketing
plannerwire.net	News, information and community
smallmarketmeetings.com	Small Market Meetings – small cities, facilities and planners
specialevents.com	Special Events
wheretraveler.com	Where Magazine – Destination information
VIRTUAL COMMUNITIES and BLOGS	
eventplanning.meetup.com	Event Planning MeetUp Groups
i-meet.com	For people who plan meetings and events
Meetingscommunity.org	A Community for the meetings professional
industrythoughts.net	Blog – Keith Johnson
michaelmccurry.net	Blog
interactivemeetingtechnology.com	Blog – Samuel Smith
conferencesthatwork.com	Blog
laramcculloch.com	Blog
blog.cvent.com	Blog
grassshackroad.com/blog	Blog
spinplanners.com/spinblog	Blog

http://www.eventsman.com/about/robert-rogers-blog/	Blog
Conventionplanit.com/blog	Blog
ENVIRONMENTAL RESOURCES	
carbonfund.org	Supports renewable energy, efficiency, and reforestation projects
cleanerandgreener.org	Event Certification for Cleaner and Greener events
clintonglobalinitiative.org	Clinton Global Initiative – inspiring change
dinegreen.com	Green Restaurant Association
ecobusinesslinks.com	Green Products and Resource Directory
ecocycle.org	Building a Zero Based Community
economicallysound.com/	Economically Sound resources for hospitality services
ecotourism.org	International Ecotourism Society
http://epa.gov/greenpower/partners/	List of businesses who support power sources that improve the environment
grrn.org	GrassRoots Recycling Network
greenhotels.com	Green Hotels Assoc. - List of Green Hotels
greenfieldpaper.com	Tree Free and Handmade Paper
greenseal.org/	Green Seals' Standard for Lodging Properties
livingtreepaper.com	Tree Free and Recycled Paper
nativeenergy.com	Carbon Offsetting
newleafpaper.com	Environmentally responsible and economically sound paper products
pacificforest.org	Forest Carbon Credits
zerowaste.com	Sound Resource Management
Travelmole.com	Asia, UK, USA travel information
treehugger.com	Web-based clearing house for information on eco issues
meetgreen.com	Environmental event planners and policy makers and training
ecobambooware.com	Dining ware
greenlodgingnews.com	Online newsletter

Appendices

Tips to Becoming a
Great Planner

Many people come into the meeting, event and hospitality industry by accident or by reasons other than choice. Without education or experience, how does one become a great event planner?

The event planning industry is always growing and changing. It is a vibrant, exciting industry. In the United States alone, there are about 350,000 professional event planners. These numbers are growing as the industry is becoming a more recognizable profession. In the last 35 years, meeting and event planning has created associations and affiliations with their own set of standards, procedures and certifications, making the profession viable and ethical. The meeting industry has a multitude of organizations and affiliations that offer products and services to planners.

The industry is growing because the world is holding more meetings and events than ever. There will always be events that need an experienced and dedicated planner.

Associations and Organizations

Planning associations, organizations and affiliations are dedicated to providing continuing education, conferences and seminars on the latest trends, books and newsletters. They are also valuable places for networking, and they offer many other important services.

Becoming a member of one of these organizations is not required to be a meeting planner, but it is important that you know that they exist and what they have to offer.

> **Note:** We are not recommending any of these organizations in particular; we are just informing you of their existence.

The most respected associations today are:

- Meeting Professionals International (MPI)
- Certified Meeting Planners (CMP)
- Professional Convention Management Association (PCMA)
- American Society of Association Executives (ASAE)

Others Include:

- Certified Special Events Professional (CSEP)
- International Special Events Society (ISES)
- Certification in Meeting Management (CMM)

There are associations tailored to specific market segments such as corporate, association, government and special events. Some are on the international, national, state or local levels. Before you join, make sure that these associations have value for you and your specific field of planning. Membership fees can be expensive.

Some of the value they offer you:

- Networking
- Continuing education
- Events
- Certification

- Reference access
- Credibility
- Employment opportunities
- Contacts around the world

Networking is high on the list of values. Having access to people and places in the industry is golden. You never know when you will need a resource at a moment's notice. If event planning is your career path, be active whenever you can, get involved and be a resource for others.

Trade Publications

Publications offer another great tool for keeping up with the industry trends. These magazines often contain articles on job opportunities, destination options, salary information, hotel and resort data, industry best practices, meeting and planning strategies, contracting and legal information, and who's who in the business.

Some associations have trade publications as a part of their membership.

Qualities of an Event Planner

The role of event coordinator is a demanding one. Your responsibilities change from day to day and from minute to minute. You must be able to remember details, manage personnel, plan a budget, administer and coordinate multiple activities, have some marketing knowledge, and have good administration skills. A few necessary traits of a great planner are:

- **Organizational skills and an eye for detail** – An event planner should be detail-oriented with the ability to make a comprehensive plan of attack, someone with good time management skills, the ability to keep an activity log, create and follow timelines, concentrate on results, do what is important, set daily goals, and make priority lists.

- **Develop and maintain interpersonal relationships** – The ability to build good relationships is critical. These relationships may include your clients, staff, servers, balloon company, director of operations and the CEO of a Fortune 500 company. Having the ability to communicate with each of these diverse types of people and personalities will make for strong relationships.

- **Have great written and oral communication skills** – You must be articulate and professional. Verbal communication and good writing skills are necessary. The ability to read non-verbal signals and the ability to listen and pay attention are very useful and important skills. Also, it is important to be willing and confident enough to ask questions.

- **Creativity** – A creative person can offer the unexpected and be unique, can brainstorm with others involved, discuss all ideas, pay attention to the latest fads, and keep informed on trends of the trade.

- **Levelheaded and a quick thinker** – Having the ability to work under pressure goes a long way in this business. No matter how organized you are, something will unexpectedly come up, and it will be your job to solve the problem quickly and quietly. It is the nature of the business. You need to have the skill to remain calm and think on your feet.

- **Determination and Persistence** – Never settle for the status quo. Be persistent with people who can get you what you need – permits, for example. Do not be afraid to call in the big guns when needed.

- **Good negotiation skills** – Negotiation is very important for both you and your client. You need to be able to negotiate your fee and vendor prices. Making it a win-win situation for everyone involved is the key. Knowing the right person to negotiate with is crucial, as well as having the appropriate knowledge of what the right prices are in that industry. If they will not negotiate with money, there may be other things worth negotiating for, such as extra rooms, free parking or an additional meeting room for your office at a conference. Just remember to ask for what you want!

Negotiations Skills and Strategies

"In business, you do not get what you deserve; you get what you negotiate."
Chester Karrass, Founder of Effective Negotiating™

Knowing how to get what you want is a key attribute for an event planner. Negotiating is an acquired skill that can be improved with experience.

A good negotiator has the ability to get more money, get extra of what they want, have productive relationships, head off misunderstandings and settle conflicts that may arise. A planner does all this in a professional and effective way with all types of people.

Negotiating is an integral part of our daily lives, even if we are not aware of it. A good negotiator can get to the point quickly and astutely, saving time and money. Here are a few strategies to hone your negotiation skills:

- Look at both sides of the deal when asking for changes. Make sure that the end result has benefits for both parties. It is an exchange of value.
- Negotiate in stages. Do not ask for everything right up front. It is definitely a process.
- Know what you want, where you can compromise, what you can give up and have alternatives when making the deal.
- Know what the alternative is before you begin negotiating.
- Seek to understand the other side's position by knowing what they want, knowing what is important to them and knowing what options the other side possesses.
- Come to the table fully armed with as much information as possible.

- Give enough information to the other party that they can make appropriate decisions.
- Find a favorable middle ground.
- Do not be emotional about the outcome.
- Ask for it all, and look good when you can compromise by letting a few things go.
- Do not accept the first offer. Make a counter offer.
- Negotiate with the appropriate decision maker from the beginning.
- Be open to splitting the difference instead of accepting a solid no.
- Leave the sticky issues till last. Focus on the easier issues first.

Potential Employers

There are hundreds of businesses that are in need of event and meeting planning specialists. The job opportunities are endless. Here is a partial list:

Event planning companies

- **Incentive Houses** – They specialize in developing programs to motivate employees.

- **Destination Management Companies** – They provide local event planning services for companies that want to hold an event in a city other than their own. They handle all the on-site details for the group. They are hired for their local knowledge and resources to plan tours, meetings, concerts, festivals, conventions, etc.

- **Event Planning Firms** – You can find local event planning company listings at your chamber of commerce or on the Internet.

- **Public Relations Firms** – Ask if event planning is part of their service because not all PR firms handle events.

- **Advertising Agencies** – Similar to PR firms, not all advertising agencies handle event planning. Some agencies that are full service will do some event planning.

Hospitality industry

The hospitality industry offers many job opportunities in the event industry. Jobs in the hospitality industry usually provide services to event planners. There are a variety of jobs in this industry and may include a combination of services.

- **Hotels and Resorts** – Hotels and resorts host numerous events: banquets, conferences, business meetings and weddings. Sales and catering, sales and marketing, or sales manager positions offer experience in event planning. Whether it is booking rooms or helping to select menus for a party, there is valuable experience in hotels and resorts.

- **Tourism Organizations** – Convention and Visitor Bureaus (CVB) act as a community's official destination management company and offer dozens of services. They are a resource for the event planner. Working for a CVB will get you unlimited contacts and experience in the event planning arena.

- **Clubs** – These types of destinations can be a great place to work. Some clubs have in-house event planners while others hire outside consultants. Clubs host numerous types of events. Some clubs where you can get event planning experience are country clubs, cultural centers, golf clubs, military clubs, private clubs, university faculty clubs and yacht clubs.

- **Cruise Lines** – Many staff members work on dry land, but there are jobs that are actually onboard. It is another great resource for getting event planning experience.

- **Vendors** – Vendors and suppliers offer a variety of job opportunities. These positions will give you the chance to assist clients in planning events. Some of these include caterers, audiovisual, technology and party rental companies.

- **Attractions** – Any place that attracts tourists will offer event planning opportunities. Many hold events to promote themselves or rent out their facility for events. Some attractions are amusement parks, aquariums, casinos, family fun centers, factory tours, ghost towns, historic sites, monuments, museums, national and state parks, performing arts, professional sports teams, raceways, scenic trains, theme parks, visitor centers, wineries, and zoos.

The corporate market

The corporate market includes corporations, associations, non-profit organizations, educational institutions, governmental offices and hospitals. You can work for one of these businesses as a meeting planner, in administration, corporate communications, human resources, marketing, member relations, or public relations.

- **Corporations** – Most large corporations have in-house event departments and staff. In smaller companies events usually fall to the office manager or someone in human resources. Occasionally they may hire out.

- **Trade and Professional Associations** – This market offers tremendous opportunities for event planners. These are many groups with a common interest that hold annual conventions, education conferences and a variety of other events.

- **Non-Profits** – This is another incredible market for event planners. Non-profits are continuously holding fundraisers and other special events.

- **Government** – There is an incredible market for event planners in government. All types of events are planned by cities, states, the federal government and individual departments. Keep in mind the political arena and all the events produced around election time.

- **Educational Facilities** – Schools, colleges and universities are another great market for event planners. Consider homecoming events, fundraisers, alumni activities, groundbreaking festivities, conferences, seminars and symposiums.

Checklists

The following checklists are only examples. Each and every event will vary. Change the activities and tasks to reflect your unique and special event. You may require a checklist that is not an example listed here. Just copy the format and create a new list for your specific topic.

Planning Session Questionnaire - high level

Here are some initial questions you can ask the planning session participants at the beginning of the planning process to uncover and develop your vision for the event. Create more questions based on your particular and unique event structure and requirements.

What is your event's primary emphasis, the overall vision? Is it education, fun, product release, fundraising, anniversary celebration? Elaborate. _____
_____

Who is the beneficiary? Will this event be for the participants, the organization or someone/something else? _____
_____

How important is financial success? Is our main focus profit, benevolence or public relations? _____
_____

What information will you be sharing, or what will you be celebrating? _____
_____

What location will serve our needs? _____
_____

Where are most of our participants located? Will they have to travel? Do we need a popular destination? _____
_____

Will money be an issue for the participants to travel? _____
_____

What is the target date? (Is it determined by the month, season, year or day of week?) _____

_____

Who is your target audience? Are they our employees, family, club members, sales team, like-minded people, industry groups or students? _____

_____

Why do they want to attend? Is it education, fun, entertainment, interest, job requirement? _____

_____

Is the event required attendance or will they be paying? _____

_____

Can they afford to attend? Who will pay for their registration, travel, lodging and other expenses? _____

_____

What is your budget? Is this a rate-conscious group? Are we making a profit? _____

_____

What kind of space is required? (Is it luxury, business, economy, fun or adventure?)

_____

_____

Will we need sponsors? Do we need to find additional funding? _____

_____

Is this a repeat event? If so, what were the results of the last event? Is there past data? What do we need to do differently? _____

_____

Will the attendees be repeats? Did they attend our past events? What evaluations were received? _____

_____

Is networking an important component? _____

_____

Have we talked about and decided on our social media components? _____

_____

Are exhibits a component, either as a source of revenue or information? _____

_____

Will there be off-site events? If so, what are they, and what is needed to make them happen? _____

_____

Have we incorporated giving back to a particular cause? Have we discussed social responsibility? _____

_____

How does environmental planning contribute to all of our decisions? _____

_____

Have we done our best to make environmental choices? _____

_____

Designing and Defining Your Event

✓	Tasks	Notes	Due Date
	Design agenda for pre-planning meeting		
	Schedule and have pre-planning meeting		
	Confirm defined purpose		
	Identify your goals and objectives		
	Confirm financial goals		
	Create environmental standards		
	Define roles and responsibilities		
	Begin talking about the budget		
	Begin to develop timelines and checklists		
	Decide what information will be shared		
	Pick your target dates		
	Develop an agenda, format and outline		
	Define type of site required		
	Research site locations		
	Define type of event to have		
	Identify participants and their demographics		
	Decide how to get message out		
	Break down tasks/assignments		
	Create committees		
	Begin talking about promotional materials and methods		
	Decide how to get our message out		
	Determine how to set your fee		
	Decide if outside vendors need to be hired		
	Decide if outside coordination help is needed		
	Make a list of potential speakers/entertainers		
✓	Create request for proposal (RFP) for venues		

Task Status Report

Event Location:	Dates of Event:
Type of Event:	Coordinator:
Beginning Date of Report:	End Date of Report:

Activity	Start Date	Complete Date	Person Responsible	Notes	Status
Create Agenda					
Select Faculty/Speaker/ Entertainment					
Select Destination					
Select Site					
Start Budget					
Work on Travel/Transportation needs					
Decide what type of Marketing is needed					
Begin Design and Printing of Marketing					
Assign Social Media and Networking Platforms and Duties					
Write Environmental Standards					
Assign Roles and Responsibilities					
Initiate Publicity/Public Relations					

Activity	Start Date	Complete Date	Person Responsible	Notes	Status
Work on Audiovisual needs					
Create Committees					
Choose a Cause to sponsor or endorse					
Begin decision-making on Food and Beverage					
Prepare room assignments and setup					
Start designing Event Materials					
Decide what type of Advertising is needed					
Enhance Website or Create new one					
Design Registration Forms					
Design Tickets and form method for Ticket Sales					
Hire Outside Help if needed					
Create Contracts					
Hire Security					
Decide on Gifts or no gifts					
Decide/Hire Photographer					
What do we need to rent					
Start Designing Signage					

Budgeting Costs and Expenses

Here is a list of expenses to get you started. Some will be appropriate for your event, and some expenses are not included here. Create your own list to suit your unique event.

Activity / Items	Estimate Cost	Actual Costs
Accommodations		
Activities – extracurricular		
Administrative overhead		
Advertising		
Audiovisual equipment		
Awards		
Bartenders		
Communications – cell phones, tablets, computers		
Entertainment		
Food and Beverage		
Freight and Shipping		
Furniture/electronic rentals		
Gifts for speakers, VIPs, volunteers		
Insurance		
Labor Charges		
Legal Services		
Lodging for speakers/VIPs		
Meeting Planner Fees		
Personnel/Staffing		
Photographer/Photography		
Postage/Mailing		
Promotional Materials/Printing		
Public relations		
Registration Materials		

Activity / Items	Estimate Cost	Actual Costs
Registration Service/Ticket service		
Security		
Set-up and take down		
Signage/Decorations		
Speakers/Faculty/Entertainers		
Staging, Lighting and Special Effects		
Supplies		
Tables and Chairs		
Taxes		
Technicians		
Transportation		
Travel for speakers/VIPs		
Venue Deposits and Costs		
Website Design		

Site Selection

✓	Tasks	Notes
	Create request for proposal and send out to prospective venues	
	Obtain several bids from several sites.	
	Arranged site visits with sites that meet your criteria.	
	Does venue have adequate space for both meeting and sleeping?	
	Is there available function space?	
	Do they meet your environmental standards?	
	What kind of food and beverage services on-site?	
	Do they have audiovisual services and technicians on-site?	
	Is the venue close to other attractions?	
	Is there ample parking?	
	Are the rates within our budget?	
	Do they have comfortable sleeping rooms?	
	Are they close to airport?	
	Do they have a pool, spa, weight room?	
	What kind of transportation is available?	
	Are they recommended by the Convention and Visitors Bureau?	
	Get a copy of menus and Food and Beverage services?	
	Are there any renovations going on during our dates?	
	Does your venue have enough meeting room space?	
	Are there hotels close by for overflow?	
	Are there adequate flights available to city?	
	Restaurants on-site or in the vicinity?	
	Do they have a shuttle from/to airport? Cost or free?	
	Is there a Concierge on site?	

✓	Tasks	Notes
	Are they ADA compliant?	
	Do they have Room Service?	
	Do they have complimentary Wi-Fi in sleeping rooms or public areas?	
	Is the venue in a safe neighborhood?	

Speakers/Entertainer Arrangements

Once you have a verbal agreement with a faculty member or speaker, presenter or entertainer, paperwork needs to exchange hands. Create a checklist for each individual/group to help maintain organization.

✓	Tasks	Notes	Date
	Write contract/agreement and deliver for signature		
	Has the agreement/contract been signed and returned?		
	Get bios, testimonials, vitas, photos, blog site info, Twitter, Facebook, etc.		
	Is the payment agreement complete?		
	Are the audiovisual requirements discussed and finalized?		
	Are the hotel accommodations complete?		
	Send itinerary and agenda to speaker/entertainers		
	Transportation and travel information sent?		
	Copies of handouts received.		
	Discuss and negotiate selling products at the event.		
	Have you sent the speaker packet?		
	Is the evaluation form complete?		
	Has the presentation been received?		
	Find all social networking accounts for speakers and entertainers. Ask them to promote this event.		
	Decide if they will pay for travel expenses and then get reimbursed		
	Will arrangements need to be made for accompanying people?		

Sample Speaker/ Entertainer Agreement

Title of Event: _____

Date of Engagement: _____

Place of Event: _____

Date:	
Name:	Title:
Organization	Address:
City, State, Zip	
Title of Session:	Start Time:
Date of Session:	End Time:

We are excited to have you speak/present/hold workshop or entertain at our next annual _____. In exchange for your time and expertise, you will receive the following: (put in what you will offer)

Roundtrip airfare

Hotel Room for two nights – the night prior to and night of your speaking engagement

All meals for two days (or dinner, breakfast, lunch, dinner, breakfast, lunch)

Registration for entire conference

Per Diem in the amount of $_____

Speaking/Entertainment fee of $_____

We will be happy to copy your handout materials (set limit) if you provided an original to us at least two weeks prior to your presentation. We will also provide you with audiovisual equipment you may need for your presentation. (You might limit if your budget is tight). You may add your environmental standard here if you have one regarding handout usage, such as 2-sided printing on recycled paper or keeping number of pages down, etc.

Please send us your bio/vita to include in our promotion material as soon as possible.

Let us know soon your audiovisual requirements. Check the following items needed. Please be specific, and only choose what you will really need. If you will be using a computerized presentation, please bring your own laptop.

- ❑ Internet Connection / Wi-Fi
- ❑ LCD projector
- ❑ Overhead projector and screen
- ❑ Slide projector
- ❑ Wireless Microphone
- ❑ DVD and monitor
- ❑ Flipchart
- ❑ Other _____

You are responsible for making your airline reservations and taxi/shuttle arrangements. We will make the hotel reservations for you. Enclosed is a working draft of the agenda for the conference.

I – speaker, hereby agree to present at the <name of meeting>. I affirm that, to my knowledge, none of the material presented, either verbally or in written materials, infringes upon any copyright or any person's right of privacy. I will not libel or slander any other person, facility, company, product or service during my presentation. If such affirmation is breached, I indemnify and hold harmless <insert company> and all contracted service providers.

I also understand I cannot make a "sales pitch" or I can make a sales pitch and sell books for any specific firm, publication or service during my presentation. I can provide participants with an opportunity to purchase publications or materials at the conclusion of my session.

_____I agree to have my session webcasted or podcasted, and the sessions will be available for sale (or free) for with the proceeds going to <insert who>.

Accepted: _____

Date: _____

Print Name: _____

Please fax or mail this agreement with your bio/vita to: <phone, address>

Food and Beverage Functions

Create a checklist for each separate meal and beverage function, even if it is one coffee break in the morning and one in the afternoon. Make separate checklists because they will be different.

✓	Tasks	Notes:
	Do you know your participants likes and dislikes, wants and needs? Find out.	
	Assignment of rooms. Be sure room choice can accommodate the style of function you are having.	
	Look over menus and get bids.	
	Establish your food and beverage budget.	
	Will the price of the meal be included in the registration or separate charge?	
	Create timelines for menu planning.	
	Meet with the chef and/or catering department or company.	
	Provide catering with your agenda and timelines.	
	Decide styles of service: ❑ Buffet ❑ Reception ❑ Sit-down ❑ Formal/informal ❑ Free/limited pour for receptions	
	For cocktail reception: ❑ Buffet or served ❑ Bar setup; how many bartenders? ❑ Charge/not charge and how for liquor	
	Determine theme/decorations.	

✓	Tasks	Notes:
	Other considerations for food functions: ❑ Know the liquor laws ❑ Checkrooms ❑ Microphones or audiovisuals ❑ Staging ❑ Table cars ❑ Printed menus ❑ Gifts ❑ Head table ❑ Reserved tables	
	Breaks needed for a.m. and p.m. – How many?	
	What to serve at breaks? Think healthy?	
	Will outside vendors be needed?	
	How to ask guests what special dietary needs they may have?	
	What kind of seating arrangement is needed?	
	Arrange with the catering a pre-event meeting.	
	Decide number of staff or volunteers needed.	
	How much ice needed, if outside?	
	Take into consideration our environmental standards when choosing menu and drinks	
	What to do with leftover food?	
	Have we looked at cost-cutting suggestions?	
	What equipment is needed for an outside event? ❑ Tents ❑ Heaters ❑ Lighting ❑ Etc.	
	What is the parking situation? For catering people and for guests?	
	Do we need to hire parking attendants?	

Quick Reference Guide for Food and Beverage Serving Amounts

Keep these formulas handy to quickly satisfy the food and beverage needs of your participants.

Coffee Breaks and Continental Breakfasts

Morning	Afternoon	Coffee
❑ 65% hot ❑ 35% cold beverages ❑ 50-75% diet soft drinks ❑ 25% regular soft drinks	❑ 35% hot ❑ 65% cold beverages ❑ 50-75% diet soft drinks ❑ 25% regular soft drinks	❑ 18-20 cups per gallon ❑ 14-16 cups per gallon (mugs) ❑ 60% regular/40% decaf

Alcohol Service

The following amounts are standard, and they will change depending on your specific group.

- Three bottles per table of eight (2 white & 1 red) with dinner
- Five 5 oz. glasses per 750 ml bottle
- Ten 5 oz. glasses per 1.5 liter magnum
- One half bottle per person with a 10 percent cushion
- Consumption of white wine is higher in the summer and red wine in the winter
- For every 10 bottles of white or sparkling wine have 2 bottles of red (opposite if red meat is your entree)
- Your wine cost should not exceed 20 percent of the total food and beverage cost
- You will get 21-25 drinks per bottle of liquor

- If you serve both hard liquor and beer and wine, count on 50 percent of the group wanting one or the other
- Women consume more wine than liquor
- Cash Bar – after a meeting: 50 percent will stay and have 1.5 drinks (1 hour reception)
- Hosted Bar – Cocktail Hour: 80 percent will stay and have 2 to 2.5 drinks in 1 hour and 3 to 3.5 drinks in 1.5 hours

Receptions

- 6–8 hors d'oeuvres pieces per person per hour if reception is prior to dinner
- 10–12 hors d'oeuvres pieces per person per hour if reception is in place of dinner
- Typical wine consumption is three glasses during a 2-hour reception

Room Set-up and Audiovisual Needs

Create a checklist for each separate room where audiovisual needs are required.

✓	Tasks	Notes:
	Talk with speakers/entertainers about their needs	
	Talk with and/or meet with audiovisual and technical department	
	Received bids from outside vendors	
	Put all costs in budget	
	Review and sign contracts	
	Decide what you need and how many: ❑ Internet Access / Wi-Fi ❑ LCD Projector ❑ Slide Projector ❑ Overhead Projectors ❑ Microphones (what kinds) ❑ Panel table/Podium ❑ Staging ❑ Movie Projector ❑ Wide Screens ❑ Spotlights ❑ Special Effects ❑ Easel Pad and markers ❑ Audio or video taped sessions ❑ Webcasting or podcasting ability ❑ Simulcasts needed for additional rooms	
	What are your lighting needs?	
	Do you need walkie talkies or cell phones?	
	Speak with the Banquet team for room setup ❑ Rounds ❑ Theatre ❑ Classroom ❑ U-shaped ❑ Banquet ❑ Conference ❑ Reception ❑ Staging	

Room Setup Matrix Example

The following matrix can be used when all food and beverages, room setup and audiovisual equipment requirements are known. This is a good reference table to use for you, your volunteers, the venue and staff.

Date of Event:

Room Name	Time	Event type and Speaker	Room Setup	Audiovisual	Food and Beverage Ordered
Marin A Check room at 10:30 am	11 a.m. – 2 p.m.	Lunch – Keynote speaker Ms. Cagan	Rounds for 100 13 tables with linens 8 chairs per table	2 lavaliere mics • Stage • Podium • 2 rectangle tables with skirt • Internet access • LCD Projector • Handouts	Lunch for 100 • Chicken with veggies • Ice Tea and Lemonade
Sonoma B	8 a.m. – 5:30 p.m.	Meeting Ms. Saks	Theatre Style	Internet access • LCD Projector • Podium • Easel and Pad with markers	N/A
Foyer in front of Sonoma B and Napa C	Break at 10:30 – 11:00 a.m.	Coffee break at 10:30	4 8' rectangles with skirts	N/A	2 gallon coffee • 1 gal decaf • 1 gal hot water with tea bags • 5 dozen Danish
Napa C	8 am – 5:30 pm	Meeting Ms. Currey Ms. Lord Ms. Cadigan	Classroom Style	Internet access • LCD Projector • Podium / mic • Overhead Projector • 1 lavaliere mic	N/A
Marin A	5pm – 10 pm	Dinner and panel Mr. Morgan Ms. Daly Mr. McGreen Ms. Shaw Ms. Lublin	Rounds 13 tables with linens – blue napkins and flower bouquet 8 chairs per table	2 lavaliere mics • 2 table top mics • Stage • Podium • 4 rectangle tables with skirts	Dinner for 100 • Steak with asparagus • Ice Tea • 2 bottles red wine per table • 1 bottle white wine per table • Orange sherbet for dessert.

Registration Setup

✓	Tasks	Notes
	Develop registration system or select suitable registration software with appropriate database functions.	
	Enter data: Conference name, dates, location, tracks, social events, exhibitors, speakers	
	Enter registrants: name, company, address, telephone, email, fee payment method	
	Decide payment process for deposit, credit cards, checks, etc.	
	Forward confirmation, acknowledgements, and/or appropriate communications regarding receipt of registration	
	For those who owe money, prepare special correspondence on a regular basis until paid or in accordance with the stated agreement	
	For cancellations, refunds and other customer services, retrieve records, enter requested charges, acknowledge and process refund if required	
	Print badges (right before event)	
	Prepare on-site registration lists	
	Prepare and/or include in on-site packages the certifications of attendance	
	Prepare/train on-site registration staff, adhering to policies	
	Review on-site logistics, signage and traffic flow	
	Prepare a help desk	
	Prepare supply of registrations forms for on-site registration for walk-ins	
	Process on-site registrations	
	Process all monies collected on-site	
	Check collections and do cleanup: letters to no-shows and to those who still owe money	
	Do the final accounting, reconciliation and reports	

Designing Your Promotional Material

Remember to create material with attention, interest and desire. Make sure to promote the action and use strong and inviting verbiage.

✓	Tasks	Notes
	Name event	
	Prepare a budget for promotional materials	
	Decide the methods of promotion and create material for each style	
	Create Checklists and Timelines for materials	
	Find printer and or web designer – get bids	
	Assign a social media guru	
	Look into professional mailing companies	
	Begin designing material	
	Decide on artwork and colors	
	Design logo if needed	
	Prepare production schedule	
	Create registration form or sign-up sheets both for web and paper	
	Proof and then proof again all the material	
	Decide method of promotion ❑ Social networking/media ❑ Mailing Lists ❑ Email Lists ❑ Brochure ❑ Advertising ❑ Flyers ❑ Telephone solicitation ❑ Save the date cards	
	Send material to printer either by hard copy or electronically	
	Sort, distribute, deliver, mail, pass out, email, etc. promotions.	
	Have system for immediate RSVPs for registration or ticket sales.	

Social Media/Networking/Marketing

✓	Tasks	Notes
	Set up strategy for your social media and social networking	
	Create a website for your event if you don't already have one	
	Decide platforms for networking and marketing. Know what each does, and decide whether or not this platform will enhance your event. Here are a few options to look into: ❑ Facebook ❑ Twitter ❑ LinkedIn ❑ Instagram ❑ YouTube ❑ Reddit ❑ Digg ❑ Foursquare ❑ Google Buzz ❑ Google+ ❑ Flickr ❑ Pinterest	
	Choose Media Guru to handle or keep track of sites and feeds	
	Create blog and become a blogger	
	Set up accounts on various media sites	
	Decide when to start (today?)	
	Join other groups associated with event planning and the type of event you are producing	
	Decide if you want a virtual meeting	
	Plan a series of podcasts or videos for YouTube	
	Find bloggers to follow	
	Decide what other technology to have at the event to gain a wider audience	
	Advertise or just participate?	

Environmental Checklist for Venue Selection

This list is quite extensive, but when you have created your own environmental standards you will know which of the following questions and answers pertain to you.

Item/Question	Yes	No	Notes
Does property purchase reusable, recycled and durable products or products that can be recycled?			
Does property have an in-house recycling program for both the property and guests? What materials are collected?			
Does property recycle any other materials (linens, phone books, oil, pallets, batteries, etc.)?			
Will your property provide recycling bins for the meeting? What materials will have recycling bins: aluminum, glass, newspaper, white paper, plastic, steel cans?			
Will property commit to seeing that the above items collected from our meeting are actually recycled?			
Does property have a contract with recycling hauler or business?			
Does property donate, sell or recycle old "durables" (i.e., furnishings, etc.)?			
Will your food and beverage services use reusable items such as cloth, glass, ceramic, etc., rather than disposable items such as Styrofoam or plastic for our meeting?			
Will your property use cream pitchers, sugar pourers and washable spoons rather than individual creamer and sugar packets, etc., for our meeting? Jelly servers rather than individual packets? Other?			
Will your kitchen purchase fresh rather than packaged produce?			
Are vegetarian, vegan and other special menus available?			

Who pays for bottle deposits – the client or the property?			
Does your property donate leftover food to a local nonprofit organization?			
Will you provide cloth rather than disposable table drapes for display tables?			
Does your property have props, decorations, foliage or centerpieces that you can use?			
Will your property use chips or coins rather than disposable paper tickets for coat checking and auto parking?			
Does your property have guestroom dispensers for soap and shampoo?			
Is property willing to remove all small plastic amenity bottles from the guest rooms that our participants will occupy?			
Does property give guests a choice on having bath linens and bed sheets exchanged?			
Do guest rooms have low-flow showerheads? Low-flow sink aerators?			
Will pitchers of water be placed on the tables rather than pre-pouring glasses of water?			
Will you use insulated water containers to keep the water cold longer?			
Will you use water from a cooler rather than using ice?			
Will you use leftover water and ice to water plants and replenish fountains?			
What other water conservation measures have been taken?			
What are you doing to reduce dry cleaning and laundry paraphernalia?			
Does property offer double-sided copying at a reduced rate?			
Do doors to your meeting rooms open and close silently, without any sound?			

At the close of our meeting, is your property willing to distribute meeting materials and sample products left behind to a local charity that can put them to good use?			
What percentage of your property's lighting is fluorescent?			
Do meeting rooms have dimmers on lights?			
Do meeting rooms have windows for natural lighting?			
What other energy conservation measures have been taken?			
What other conservation measures have you incorporated?			
Is there anything further in regards to being "green" that your property will offer us?			

Planning for a Cause – Social Responsibility

This is a topic that should be discussed and decided by the powers that be... Find a cause to help that matches the values of your company/business and will be important to your audience.

✓	Tasks	Notes
	Have a meeting with the management, client or top dog.	
	Find out what charities, local entities or national causes the company already works with.	
	Discuss what might be important to the participants.	
	Decide if something with activity can be done during event.	
	Raise money or awareness (or both).	
	Contact those organizations you've chosen in the city you will be holding event.	
	Choose someone to be responsible for this portion of the event.	
	Write copy that will go in marketing material.	
	Plan the event within the event.	
	Notify the participants of the plan.	
	Contact a person to represent cause at the event	

Sample Evaluation Form

Was the information presented useful to you?	❏ Yes ❏ No
Was the class/seminar/workshop what you had expected?	❏ Yes ❏ No
Was the handout material relevant and covered the subject?	❏ Yes ❏ No
Did the instructor/speaker have sufficient knowledge of the topic?	❏ Yes ❏ No
How would you rate the overall class/workshop/seminar?	❏ Excellent ❏ Good ❏ Fair ❏ Poor
Topics not covered that you would like to learn about?	
Suggestions for improvement:	
Would you be interested in seminars on different aspects of this topic?	❏ Yes ❏ No
Do you want to be on our mailing list?	❏ Yes ❏ No
Name:	
City/State/Zip:	
Phone:	
Email address:	

Post Event Fact Status Sheet

✓	Statistics	Notes
	Name of Event:	
	Event Coordinator(s):	
	Defined Purpose:	
	Goals and Objectives:	
	Dates:	
	Destination:	
	Venues:	
	Number of participants:	
	Sleeping rooms used:	
	Transportation used:	
	Theme:	
	Food and beverage used:	
	Marketing efforts:	
	Fees for participants:	
	Budget:	
	Speakers:	
	Topics:	
	Agenda:	
	Meeting rooms:	
	Exhibits:	
	Special Events:	

APPENDIX

C

Timelines

Timelines can be used to set up and keep you organized for the event itself. Another way to use timelines is for each category similar to the ones that you have created checklists for. You can create a timeline for food and beverage, another for audiovisual equipment, etc. The checklists make sure you have all your bases covered, but the timelines can assist you to get it all done in a timely manner. Create your own timelines for each area you will be working on to be more successful.

Timeline for a smaller events

Make sure all the tasks connected with your type of event are included. Make it as comprehensive as possible.

Timeframe	To Do List / Tasks	Date ✓	Notes
3 months out (Put in actual dates)	Hold committee/staff meeting – define goals and objectives, financial goals – Defined vision		
	Review Roles and Responsibilities		
	Create Budget, define audience		
Ten weeks out	Secure Site/facility, sign contracts		
	Start promotional material		
Nine weeks	Secure Speaker or Entertainment		
Eight weeks	Start preparing menus		
	Design layout		
Seven weeks	Determine Meeting Format		
	Complete contract agreements		
	Edit promotional material		
Six weeks	Approve promotional material		
	Secure travel arrangements/ information		
	Order food and beverage (f/b) and audiovisual (a/v) needs		
Five weeks	Print material and send out/place ad/ put up flyers, write blog		
	Make travel arrangements for speakers/staff		
	Secure sleeping rooms		
Four weeks	Buy name badges/gifts/memorabilia		
	Confirm number of participants to appropriate people		
	Order flowers/decorations		

Timeframe	To Do List / Tasks	Date ✓	Notes
Three weeks	Pay all deposits required		
Two weeks	Confirm participants		
	Finalize order for f/b and a/v		
	Finalize any travel arrangements		
	Create name badges/lists and signage		
One week out	Ship materials to site		
	Send final numbers of participants for f/b, a/v		
	Rehearse on-site personnel		
	Review all confirmations		
	Confirm numbers again to all appropriate parties (caterer, hotel, speaker or birthday girl)		
Day before	Review all events, do a run through		
	Establish on-site presence		
	Hold pre-conference with faculty		
	Check to see if all your materials have arrived		
	Set up Registration		

Large Event Timeline

Coordination of very large events will sometimes begin two to three years in advance, especially when booking a venue and entertainment. Just change the dates accordingly and create a timeline that is unique to your event.

Timeframe	To Do List / Tasks	Date ✓	Notes
1 year out (Put in your actual dates)	Hold committee/staff meeting, define goals and objectives, create roles and responsibilities		
	Choose Destination – City, State		
	Define audience – participants		
	Meet with Event Planner and others to review Roles and Responsibilities		
	Confirm Financial goals and objectives		
	Prepare budget		
	Choose Location – venue		
	Confirm dates and times		
11 months	Conduct site inspection		
10 months	Secure facility/sign contracts		
9 months	Begin researching for speakers and entertainment		
	List subjects for agenda		
8 months	Draft topics and agenda		
7 months	Confirm speakers/entertainment		
6 months	Begin Design of Promotional Material		
	Get quotes for printed material		
5 months	Develop guest list		
	Confirm hotel		
	Edit materials		
	Start food/beverage (f/b) and audiovisual (a/v) process		

4 months	Final Design to Printer		
	Start preparing or finalize agenda		
3 months	Material to Mail House		
	Meeting with Meeting Planner and others to review roles and responsibilities		
	Review Budget		
	Determine Meeting Format		
	Complete contract agreements		
	Develop promotional material		
	Secure travel arrangements/information		
	Approve promotional material		
	Hire photographer, other services and vendors		
Five weeks	Complete meeting materials		
	Confirm volunteers and the responsibilities		
Four weeks	Order signage		
	Make sure all contracts are signed		
	Print meeting materials		
	Confirm travel arrangements for speakers/staff		
Three weeks	Complete any additional printed material		
	Review everything		
	Confirm number participants		
	Finalize f/b menus		
	Get a massage		
Two weeks out	Buy last office supplies for event		
	Finalize everything		
	Ship materials to site		
	Send final numbers for participants f/b, a/v		

One week	Prepare welcome letters, certificates		
	Print name badges		
	Rehearse on-site personnel		
	Review all confirmations		
	Prepare Tool Kit		
Night/Day before	Arrive on-site/Establish on-site presence		
	Hold pre-conference with faculty		
	Prepare volunteers – hold meeting		
	Set up registration area		
	Prepare Binder		
Day of Event	Have Tool Kit		
	Have Binders		
	Station Volunteers		
	Check all equipment and f/b lists		
After Event	Thank you notes – gifts, tips and gratuities		
	Create Final Report/Summary		
	Review and summarize evaluations		
	Review and finalize budget		
	Pay last of the bills due		

About the Author

At an early age, Shannon Kilkenny began what would become her career in event planning by gathering her neighborhood friends on a regular basis. Throughout high school and college, she volunteered for committees and headed organizations that allowed her to bring people together for a variety of reasons. Concurrently, she began a writing career with newsletters, articles, copy for marketing material, and later writing and editing guidebooks, user manuals, and how-to books. These two careers have continued in concert for more than 35 years.

Her expertise and good humor have helped to create successful business relationships with clients in the banking industry, hospitality trade, educational and non-profit organizations, professional associations, athletic clubs, and the environmental community. Having worked with these diverse groups, Ms. Kilkenny is familiar with multiple segments of the business and social world.

With her writing and event planning skills strongly embedded, using her multi-layered experiences, the book, *The Complete Guide to Successful Event Planning*, was born. Keeping up with the event planning world, she saw continuing changes for the environment, social networking and social media and decided a revised edition was necessary. Hence, Volume Three!

She is currently teaching event planning classes, workshops and seminars, and speaking at industry conferences and conventions. She developed a curriculum for all levels of commitment. She has mentored beginners through their first event and assisted seasoned professionals seeking new heights of proficiency.

In her leisure time, you will find her in her garden, in her kayak, writing a fiction novel or in the clutches of a good book. Ms. Kilkenny lives by the ocean north of San Francisco.

Mentor Moment

Lee Richter, CEO
Event Planners Association
EventPlannersAssociation.com

As an event planner for over 25 years, I have experienced dozens of changes in the hospitality industry. The biggest impact to my business growth in the last few years is social media. Social media plays an important role when building a business brand. Connecting to your ideal client is just a click away. You can share engaging and valuable information while building meaningful connections.

We have seen wedding and party photos posted on social media sites like Pinterest, Instagram and Facebook, before, during and after an event. Guests at the venue and others that missed the event have an opportunity to unite when celebrating the happy couple or the right of passage. Event planners often create an Internet campaign posting information and details leading up the event too. Clients use sites like *The Knot* and *Evite* to share ideas and to create guest interactions to upcoming festivities.

When you want your photo to get more likes and shares, it can turn into an entertaining meme by adding a quote or a funny statement. A meme can create an emotional reaction or connection to the audience. When the meme is authentic and engaging, it takes on a life of its own with shares and comments from people around the world.

In January 2016, a meme on my Facebook page went viral. It was interesting, because the meme was posted a few months earlier and I did not see an indication that it was ready to be shared with millions of people. Then people from Australia, Italy, Dubai, England, China and the United States, etc. were sharing, commenting and clicking "like". On a Friday the reach was approaching two million people. When I returned to the office on Monday, it had reached over 20 million people. Wow … I was surprised to see that kind of engagement in just a few days. We needed to do something immediately to capture the lightening in a bottle. My team brainstormed and we agreed to post an eBook related to the meme for people to opt in and to receive as a free gift.

Thousands of people entered their data to receive the eBook, and a two-way relationship began. They never heard of me, but the meme triggered an emotional response and they wanted more. They wanted to connect and to share their thoughts. It was magical and exciting. At that moment, we began to learn some lessons and wanted to do it again.

That week the reach climbed to 30 million. We watched throughout the day and were in awe of how rapid the numbers were growing. It went to 35 million and approached 40 million by Friday. We were excited and shocked to witness a 10 times increase in under a week. This was the first time I was personally involved in something with a positive impact at a global level in a mere seven days. Now, I clearly understand why celebrities and their publicity teams get hooked on sharing stories, photos and memes. Who knew it was possible for a mere mortal to add thousands of new friends from around the world and millions of likes and comments with just one simple post? It was uncharted territory and an opportunity for me to serve my community in a profound and interesting way.

What I learned from this extraordinary ride was:

1. Make a plan and be ready for anything.
2. Be prepared to respond immediately.
3. Social media connects people worldwide and can spark a thought or idea on fire.
4. Have a way to immediately capture the frenzy and dive in deeper with the people responding.
5. Have a product like my eBook to connect to those who raised their hands and asked for more. It was a way to start a more meaningful connection with me directly. I was happy to connect with people who were moved by the meme and I was interested in their feedback and their thoughts.

Next, I created a series of emails to follow up on our common interests and offer ways of support. Over the next few weeks and months, I offered more ideas and connections creating opportunities to serve them in a way I never did before. Nurturing our connection became a priority and I asked them questions to provoke ideas and to create action.

Was this process rewarding? Yes. I loved serving the community in a meaningful and creative way. It made me feel good to help people. It was exciting to connect with people in other countries and to hear their feedback.

I recognized the importance of being prepared and to respond immediately to the excitement. If they show interest; engage and share more. I suggest that you visit other sites and blogs to participate in ways that interest you and in ways to initiate remarkable connections for you and your business.

Remember that social media is a powerful way to make connections to vendors, potential customers, venues, ideas and people you may never have met any other way. In business, it is who you know that can make a big difference and in social media the connection matters more than anything.

Index